Here &
Hereafter

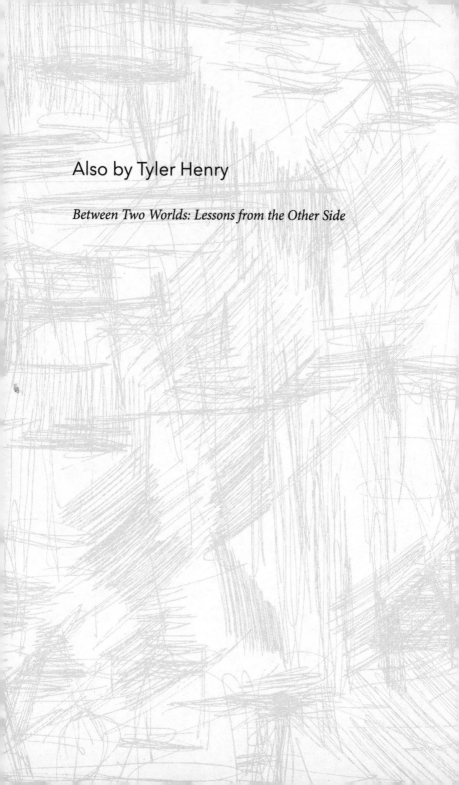

Also by Tyler Henry

Between Two Worlds: Lessons from the Other Side

Here &
Hereafter

Tyler Henry

How Wisdom from the Departed
Can Transform Your Life Now

ST. MARTIN'S
ESSENTIALS
NEW YORK

First published in the United States by St. Martin's Essentials,
an imprint of St. Martin's Publishing Group

HERE & HEREAFTER. Copyright © 2022 by Tyler Henry.
All rights reserved. Printed in the United States of America. For information,
address St. Martin's Publishing Group, 120 Broadway, New York, NY 10271.

www.stmartins.com

Designed by Jonathan Bennett

Library of Congress Cataloging-in-Publication Data

Names: Henry, Tyler, author.
Title: Here & hereafter : how wisdom from the departed can transform your
    life now / Tyler Henry.
Other titles: Here and hereafter
Description: First edition. | New York : St. Martin's Essentials, 2021.
Identifiers: LCCN 2020053243 | ISBN 9781250796776 (hardcover) |
    ISBN 9781250857392 (signed edition) | ISBN 9781250796783 (ebook)
Subjects: LCSH: Self-realization—Miscellanea. | Wisdom. | Meditations. |
    Spiritualism.
Classification: LCC BF1275.S44 H46 2021 | DDC 131—dc23
LC record available at https://lccn.loc.gov/2020053243

Our books may be purchased in bulk for promotional, educational, or business
use. Please contact your local bookseller or the Macmillan Corporate and
Premium Sales Department at 1-800-221-7945, extension 5442, or by email at
MacmillanSpecialMarkets@macmillan.com.

First Edition: 2022

10 9 8 7 6 5 4 3 2 1

Contents

Author's Note

Scribbling is a helpful tool during readings. It allows me to have a mechanism of switching on and off. The repetitive aspect of scribbling allows me to get into a meditative mindset and block out distractions. The end results often look a little surprising, but the importance of scribbling is more about the act of mindful repetition than the scribbles themselves.

Introduction

What the Departed Would Do Differently

After I had a premonition of my grandmother's death when I was ten years old, the trajectory of my life changed forever. That was fourteen years ago, and the extraordinary connections I've since witnessed in readings have transformed my understanding of the universe and our role in it. Along with my own near-death experiences, I've seen firsthand the power of divine intervention in people's lives through direct signs and profound coincidences. That, along with the sentiments expressed by those who've lived and died, have drastically altered how I view life, death, and the meaning of it all.

Death, like birth, is an inevitable part of living. What we do with the time we have defines the quality of our lives and the extent of which we learn gracefully along the way. By sharing with you what I've learned from the afterlife experience, you'll find valuable tools to lead a better, more meaningful life. Despite our individual differences, all souls share commonalities. The lessons learned after death reflect our universal similarities. In

1

the words of Ram Dass, "We're all just walking each other home."

While stubbornness, ego, ignorance, and imbalance have plagued humankind from man's beginning, it is not the true nature of our souls. This dichotomy between our human-selves and soul-selves is our responsibility to recognize and integrate. As the saying goes, "You are not a physical being having a spiritual experience; you're a spiritual being having a physical experience." All is temporary; the only guarantee is change. So how can we better navigate the inevitabilities of life?

What the departed learn in the hereafter gives us insight into the meaning of life itself. Even more pragmatically, afterlife lessons help us have a more well-rounded, meaningful view of life and death. On my own path, I've been amazed by the extremely valuable life-tools that can be found in the knowledge of what the departed would do differently.

What I've learned as a medium has shown me the importance of faith. Not only does doing a successful reading require faith in myself; I must equally have faith in a realm I do not control and rely upon entirely to do my job. Through this process of internal and external faith, I've developed a trust in a higher source of information called intuition.

Living intuitively is a must for a medium, but we all have that little voice in the back of our heads that chimes in occasionally. If only we listened to it more! If we did, we'd live more efficiently, never distracted by what isn't worth our time. By knowing when to recognize opportunity, we can seize it. In this way, intuition is a powerful tool in discerning what is worth our focus and what is not. Intuition can show us paths we didn't see before and pave new ones through everything it offers us.

In seeing the process of growth reported by those who've passed away, I've noticed certain afterlife processes appear universal. No matter who you are, we all are subject to the same mechanisms of the universe. These processes directly alter our consciousness in death, giving us insight into how we lived and how we helped. These understandings acquired by those on the other side give hints as to how we can live to our fullest potential. By recognizing the perspective of the afterlife, we can shift our perspective in this one.

All understandings acquired from the other side seem to come from a process I call a life review, which ultimately leads to ego death. Much like how when a baby is born it must pass through the birth canal and the umbilical cord must be cut, our souls go through a detachment process upon entering the next realm. Through this series of events, we shed our human problems, our greatest traumas, and all of our existential baggage— but only by facing it all. Through our life review, we see how our single consciousness influenced everybody it ever crossed paths with and how our individual presence influenced the collective one. As we go through this process of self-realization, our consciousness views ourselves less as an individual, and more as a part of a greater, collective consciousness that everyone is a part of. With every interaction that gets integrated, the ego strips another layer. We realize that we're all different fingers on the same hand; we're all extensions of the same source.

Within this understanding comes acceptance. As we face how our actions helped or hurt others—and in turn ourselves—we come to terms with every issue, every roadblock, every heartbreak, and every thing that has ever crossed our path. This is the definition of true peace. I don't define heaven as a clouded place with harp-playing babies; I view it as a state that our consciousness inevitably enters and grows into. We ultimately become aware of our part of the vast network of consciousness that permeates the universe. This enlightenment makes our human problems look minor by comparison, but without human problems, this enlightenment wouldn't be possible.

I see great similarities between the state we achieve when we die and what many religions try to achieve while here on Earth. Through religion, spirituality, and mysticism, the world communicates with a higher power that mankind has always instinctively perceived as there. In the quest to reach this state, our history is steeped in ritual and practice, as we do certain things with the goal of getting more in alignment with the source. Carl Jung refers to this process of integrating the conscious and unconscious as individuation. Buddha referred to it as enlightenment. Whatever you choose to call it, there's always been an understanding that by going inward, we can resolve what we face outwardly.

I don't think it's realistic to aim for total enlightenment in our lives. It simply isn't practical in Western society. I don't believe we should destroy our ego; we should improve it. As you'll see, it's a necessary defense structure that gets us through life. Unless you're a Tibetan monk in a faraway temple, I'm hesitant to recommend striving for ascendance. Setting the bar a little lower and living in a way that is enlightening versus striving for enlightenment is an important distinction. We are all works in progress, and these lessons are aimed to be as practical as they are profound. In juggling the balance of conscious and unconscious, ego and soul, love and fear, we can find equilibrium in our often unbalanced world.

This book will provide the tools to refine your intuition, recognize your ego, and make your world a little less heavy. As you heal individually, a ripple effect emanates and inspires others to heal as well. Here the journey begins.

By learning from the experiences of those who came and went before us, we can limit our regrets by knowing when to speak up. Through intuition we can discern the world in a way that reaches far into our soul and then out into the world around us. When we listen to the whispers of the universe, we discover not only what to do, but who we are.

1

Lead a Spirit-Filled Life

The Meaning of Mystical Living

Fundamentally, living a spiritual life means that we acknowledge the mystical side of reality. Mysticism has been the common denominator between all religions and spiritualities since the beginning of time. It has never been fully understood, but that's by design. The nature of mystical experiences transcends words, and those who experience these states often spend the rest of their lives trying to understand them. Since the start, people have recognized that there is something "else" out there that makes up the fabric of existence. Early religions were based heavily on ancestor worship, which served as a communal spirituality in which mankind of the past and present were inherently linked. As time went on, polytheistic and monotheistic religions prevailed. All were attempts at looking towards the heavens for understanding on Earth. For as long as this understanding has existed, so have attempts at communicating with this "other" part of reality. This relationship is the basis of all religious practice.

Whether we're putting our hands together in prayer or reaching a state of transcendent meditation, the goal is the same: to commune with the ether and change our consciousness for the better. All spiritual practices revolve around aligning oneself with a greater force in the hopes of bettering oneself. Prayer provides a sense of being heard, and faith motivates people to reach new heights, even when they can't see them. These concepts are more than a belief. They're practices. African tribes conduct hypnotic drum circles and dances that are saved only for special moments when spiritual communication is attempted. Similarly, many of us at one time or another can relate to closing our eyes and "talking it out" internally, via prayer. Catholics repetitiously say the rosary as a way of achieving their spiritual goal, while Tibetan monks utilize singing bowls to create a repetitive, drone-like sound that helps with meditation and prayer. I emphasize these practices because they all share one thing in common: there's an element of repetition to the rituals, much like the way I scribble. Anyone who has seen me do a reading knows that it's really more about the process of scribbling that helps me connect, rather than what gets written on the page. My process of doodling is a spiritual practice to me: it's my cue to the Universe that I'm ready to work and enter into a different headspace. The repetition of the action helps me enter into an altered state of consciousness, best described as a trance. In this state, I'm still somewhat aware of my surroundings, but more able to notice spiritual impressions that might normally go ignored. The process of doing something repetitively can help us create a structure by which we can communicate with the great unseen.

Having healthy rituals is a way of separating the mundanity of life from the intensity of spiritual connection. When we create a sacred practice, or routine, we create a foundation for our spirituality to work off of. This is a fundamental concept that I encourage everyone to implement: maintain a schedule of spiritual practices. They don't have to be complicated, and in fact, it's better if they're not. Carving out time for daily meditation and prayer creates a platform for insight. When we do our part to seek out the mystical, it lends the Universe an opportunity to seek us out in return. The results can be life-changing.

Before we get much further into the discussion around mysticism, it's important to understand the characteristics of mystical experiences. The nature of these moments is profound and equally mind-boggling. They come out of nowhere and leave the recipient changed and inspired. American philosopher and psychologist William James (1842–1910) investigated religious experiences in his book *The Varieties of Religious Experience*. Though he wasn't a mystic, he looked at the evidence and concluded that mysticism was the source of all religions. He defined four characteristics of mystical states:

1. Ineffability, meaning it is inexpressible in words. The experience is so unusual that words can't accurately describe how profound it is. People may try to describe their mystical experiences, but words never truly convey the magnitude of it.

2. Noetic quality, meaning the experiencer becomes fervently fascinated by the pursuit of knowledge. More than a logical search for insight, it's motivated by deep feelings.

3. Transiency, meaning they're usually brief but meaningful.

4. Passivity, meaning the experience makes the experiencer feel overwhelmingly part of a superior force, and they may not be able to focus on anything else.

People who have experienced near-death experiences (NDEs) describe many of these traits in their own experience. Similarly, so do those who historically had religious visions and moments in which they felt divinely inspired. Regardless of your beliefs on the origin of these momentous events, they happen to people and create massive change.

From Harriet Tubman to Joan of Arc, countless historical figures credited otherworldly visitations with their world-altering accomplishments. Artist Salvador Dalí was known to regularly look at his dreams for inspiration for his surreal art. He would take advantage of the time between being awake and falling asleep to glean inspiration for his paintings. He was known to hold a spoon in his hand as he dozed off, so that the moment he entered into the half-asleep state called hypnagogia, the spoon would drop and he'd be jolted awake. Upon awakening, he'd recollect any visions or images that started to form while he was in this in-between state of consciousness. Albert Einstein was also known to routinely take twenty-minute naps as a way of going inward with the goal of coming up with new ideas. Isaac Newton, the father of modern physics, was heavily involved in the spiritual pursuit of alchemy and believed mysticism to be an extension of science. All of these individuals changed the world simply by honoring what they felt called to do. This is intuition.

The spiritual path is the pursuit of understanding universal mysteries that can't yet be entirely comprehended. Experiencers often feel that they don't have the brainpower to contextualize their experience, though it was clearly real and deeply impactful. Mystical activities are deeply personal practices aimed at finding greater meaning in life, and the path they send us down often benefits the greater good of mankind. Mysticism provides a direct link to knowledge about the nature of existence and the truth of all things.

Sometimes, it's motivated by interactions with non-human sources of insight, or a higher power. American abolitionist Harriet Tubman led slaves to freedom by following the guidance from visions she credited as being sent directly from God. Socrates referred to the Muses, unseen forces of inspiration that sometimes communicate with humans. Joseph Smith, founder of Mormonism, was compelled to create one of the most prolific modern religions through what he believed to be angelic messages. Jack Parsons, the often under-credited father of modern rocketry, revolutionized propulsion technology through intuition alone. Without a college degree, he created the fuel technology that got man to the moon.

When I was new to the world of mediumship, I made an effort to visit as many psychics and mediums as I could. I personally sat with over two hundred different spiritual practitioners, with a variety of results. I was particularly intrigued by where these individuals thought they were getting their psychic information from, and I was surprised by the variety of responses. Most acknowledged that they had spirit guides; others claimed to literally see the spirit they were talking to in the room with us. Some claimed to receive their information from other worlds, some from the Christian God, and others said they were in touch with ancient deities. It might seem easy to scoff at that idea, and the seeming disagreement between it all, but I found that this reflected the interpretational nature of spiritual connections. People projected their preconceived beliefs onto something that transcended any single individual belief.

All of these examples involve communing with higher

forces, though no one can truly agree on who exactly is sending all of these mystical moments. A Christian might perceive a mystical experience as being from Jesus, while a Spiritualist may call it a spirit. This represents the ineffable nature of mystical experiences: words fail in describing them, and we're never truly able to comprehend their origin.

It may not be our job to understand the sender of the message, as much as to put the message into action.

Mysticism encourages the conscious exploration of all concepts of reality that can be imagined. Even the most cynical scientists have a hard time maintaining a materialist view of reality after feeling the presence of the great unknown. Neurosurgeon Eben Alexander had to come to grips with a massive change of perspective after his near-death experience, eloquently described in his book *Proof of Heaven*. As it is to be expected, mystical experiences aren't taken into account by the scientific establishment, simply because they do not fall into the measurability of the scientific method. Due to their metaphysical nature, mystical experiences characteristically transcend words, reason, or rational explanations. They're indescribable, and impossible to create without the help of higher forces. With this intimate firsthand knowledge, the mystic gets closer to a spiritual union with a higher power, and an internal marriage of self results. People are forever changed once they've had a glimpse into the great hereafter. We realize we're a small piece in a bigger puzzle, and this causes irreversible shifts in perception that change how we define reality.

My own glimpse into this truth has changed how I live my life. It has drastically influenced what I prioritize and what I don't waste time with. People who have near-death experiences often describe being forever changed by an understanding of a bigger picture. They also describe often feeling motivated to share their knowledge with other people. In some ways, with every spirit I communicate with, I'm given insight into how the death process changes consciousness. This has gone on to alter how I view my own, and what I do with it with the time I have on this planet.

Living a lifestyle of alignment with the Universe strips away all of what isn't real and doesn't serve us, giving us a glimpse into our eternal nature. Living spiritually is an individual path, and only you can understand the road you're on. Whether you recognize the mystical nature of reality or not, it exists primordially and forever. The advancement of science hasn't dissuaded people from having mystical experiences, nor have science's physical explanations. Mystics have been born, are born, and will continue to be born until the end. We're not going anywhere, so we may as well take a look at the mechanisms behind the spiritual and strive to better understand them. In this path of understanding, we better understand ourselves. When you can recognize the reality of it all, life begins to change. This is the path to self-realization.

Some people feel more connected to the unseen world than others. As a medium, I often am asked if my ability is something that runs in my family. As far as I know, I'm the only one. With that said, I believe that spiritual inclinations factor in both nature and nurture. Our environment heavily shapes our receptivity to spirituality; however, we all have an individual makeup that feels called to different modalities of perspective. I heavily credit being an only child to being part of why I was able to refine my intuition. I had no one telling me otherwise. I had a lot to endeavor alone, and I was transformed through what I learned. I was a quiet child with few friends and preferred the company of adults over children. This isolative quality made me more introspective and helped me beat to my own drum without being "corrected" by others. The fact that mysticism has inspired both organized religion and alternative spirituality is a testament to the fact that human beings have always had their own interpretation of the mystical. Because of its transcendent nature, we're left to piece together what we know from what's familiar to us. This, I believe, is why there's such a disagreement and contradiction around who is the sender of the mystical: people try to attribute labels to something that cannot be simply defined and neatly categorized.

With that in mind, I think it's important to not ever

too staunchly have confidence in the origins of spiritual messages. As I am a medium, people often assume that during a reading, I'm communicating directly with a person's departed loved one. The reality is that I have a concrete relationship with what I call my guides, and they do much of the communicating on my behalf with whichever consciousness is coming through. My guides are mysterious to me, ineffable even, and I've quit trying to understand who exactly "they" are. They exist, they help me receive and send messages, and that's all that really matters to me. I urge you, too, as you go down this spiritual path, to not waste time trying to identify the sender of these profound insights. Being content with not ever fully knowing will help you recognize what you do know. The more you learn, the more you'll realize how little one person can truly understand. Our job isn't to figure it all out. We must look at what we feel called to do and what mystical experiences inspire. Our role is only to receive, to listen, and to better the world from it in our own unique way.

Much of what defines the New Age movement has a reputation for being a smorgasbord of ancient and recent belief systems, all combined into a single label that has no single doctrine. It's important to know that there is a difference between living a spiritual, non-denominational lifestyle and immersing oneself in the New Age belief systems. Much of the New Age movement derives from the New Thought Movement, an earlier ideology that encompasses metaphysics, the

Law of Attraction, personal empowerment, and the appropriation of beliefs deemed "Eastern." Basically, the European elite in the early nineteenth century had a fascination with the beliefs and practices of Tibet, India, Egypt, and other newly popularized places. The chakra system was taken from Hinduism and mixed with Buddhist philosophies. Energy healing, intuition, and yoga started replacing repentance, sin, and heaven or hell. People were fed up with fundamentalism and hellfire and wanted a more personal relationship with God. They looked to ancient religions, mythology, and lore for something to believe in. In an attempt to explore spirituality beyond the Judeo-Christian narrative, they emerged with a new mishmash of concepts.

And it stuck. New Thought was rebranded into New Age, and the sixties propelled a whole new wave of belief. Though intuition and extrasensory perception have been lumped into the New Age category, it's only because they fall into subject matter that the public currently defines as "alternative." Herein lies an example of why it's important to decondition many of the commonly accepted stereotypes around spirituality. It's much more nuanced, and interwoven, than most are willing to see. Though strides have been made in the past few decades in getting more scientific insight into what mechanisms are at play in intuition, scientists will never have an answer to the "hard problem of consciousness" until they account for the spiritual nature of reality. It's a universal truth that religion, and all of humankind, has intuitively felt drawn to, but has never been able to truly grasp. The mystical nature of reality exists no matter what we believe. Sometimes, we realize we're an extension of it.

I can't stress enough the importance of being pragmatic in the refinement of your intuition. As you lead a more spiritual life through the tools outlined in this book, it's important to make balance your main priority. Be mindful of extremes, and always be willing to change your opinion with new information. If spirituality isn't practical, then why practice it? I think it's important when dabbling in the spiritual to be wary of certainties. In my own work, I've found that the second I'm certain of something, the Universe sends a contradictory message to show me how little I actually know. For example, in the beginning of my career I believed that spirits who died recently weren't able to communicate with a medium. After doing hundreds of readings in which no one ever came through within hours or days of dying, I felt that this meant that people can't come through when they've just died. Surely, it must take time. I wrote this perspective in my first book, *Between Two Worlds*, and then went on to my daily readings. Sure enough, the first reading I did after confidently writing this sentiment down was with a woman whose father came through with crystal clarity. He had died only the day before. Talk about keeping me humble!

My point is that it's important to let the information you receive just be what it is. Notice it, document it, but don't try to label it. This will save you a lot of trouble and will help you go with the flow more easily. As human beings, we look for patterns and consistency to establish our beliefs. Mysticism throws a wrench in that. When you can go down this path with the understanding that we're only a small piece of the puzzle, and that because of that we can't fully see the whole picture, trying to understand it all becomes a lot less stressful.

Historically, communication with the divine involved meaningful coincidences, visions, and feelings that defied logic. For this reason, it's important that I stress the importance of mental stability. Balance is fundamental, and if your spirituality doesn't lead to balance, then it's not a spirituality based in equilibrium. To be able to live happily, we have to be able to take breaks from existential thinking. Using discernment with signs and hunches is key. I'm a firm believer that if you see meaning in everything, what is truly meaningful becomes meaningless. Intention is a very powerful mechanism in spirituality. It's the basis of prayer and informs everything we do. Before any action, there is intention. Our actions may have unintentional consequences, but having the ability to intend is fundamental to any conscious being. Every reading I do begins with the meeting of two intentions: mine and that of the person being read. I communicate the intentional messages relayed by those who have passed and, as I mentioned earlier, my guides. These mechanisms are no different for you than they are for me. As you work towards a more well-rounded, intuition-based life, I hope you'll be mindful of the intentions that inform your perspective.

This mindfulness is a form of intuition in itself. Through self-awareness, we can become better vehicles to reach and maximize our full potential. The more work you do internally to figure yourself out, the more connections you'll be able to make externally when they're sent to you. Synchronicity has immensely defined and guided my life, and if you're able to utilize your intuition, you'll get help you didn't even know existed.

Through the tools and concepts I'll equip you with, you'll have a full arsenal of ideas to ruminate on and decide what you resonate with. As you go down this journey of self-exploration and progress, the need for practicality is key. Growth, and spiritual journeying, can be a messy process. Feelings can come to the surface that weren't there before, and not everyone may share your enthusiasm for self-development. That's okay. Applying your spirituality and being open to what it has to teach is a deeply personal process that only you need to understand.

Your spirituality and intuition should inspire you to take a call to action, not paralyze you with fear. I receive many emails from parents who say they think their child is a medium. I ask them what they've seen to indicate this, and the story is generally the same. Usually their child says that they're seeing scary things, not wanting to sleep alone, or avoiding going to school because of what they're experiencing. Generally, I find that people assume being a child medium is scary. I can count on one hand the number of disturbing moments I had as a child with a spiritual awareness. The truth is that 95 percent of these cases are anxious children with big imaginations and parents who are taking them a little too seriously. We have to actively unlearn what we've been taught from movies and pop culture about mediums, and spiritual communication in general. It shouldn't be trivialized as a spooky thing that goes bump in the dark, and yet this popular idea of spirit communication continues. I say this, because it's important to apply this mentality to your own spiritual pursuits. Demystify any fear you have of the mystical, because if you don't, it'll block your pursuit of it. The spiritual world is a part of nature, just as existent as the environment we live in. Though the word "supernatural" defines this subject in the eyes of the public, it is simply nature that is not yet understood. Someday, it will be. Through your own work in refining intuition, recognizing it, and bringing it to the surface, you might help in changing that narrative.

It's important to give weight to logic, reason, and critical thinking. This is why I put such an emphasis on validation in a reading of information that can only be known to the person receiving the reading and the spirit coming through. Anybody can tell you your loved one is proud of you, but it's the facts and specific details that define a well-connected reading. In the same vein, we must maintain a balanced approach to any belief system we adopt, and we must see both sides. Always look at opposing arguments. Mysticism, and by extension spirituality, are sometimes perceived as intangible, impractical, or vague by people who take the materialist approach. They are none of that. I argue that intuition has informed many great accomplishments and inventions. As humans, we have always reached for the stars to understand what created us, and there's a reason for that. Spirituality takes us on journeys, leads us into explorations, and encourages us to reach new heights. Mystical people are the revolutionaries of their time, even if they don't call themselves mystics. Notable inventors, composers, philosophers, and civil rights activists have all been inspired to follow their soul's call to contribute something for humans in the future. The Xerox machine, or photocopier, was born when a channeled message was given to its inventor, Chester Carlson, during a medium reading. He was so inspired by this experience that he donated the proceeds from his life's work to psychic research. From ideological movements to utilities we use in daily life, something created the idea in the mind of the inventor. That spark of insight, that moment of epiphany, can only be credited as intuition.

The same intuition that has been used knowingly and unknowingly by the world's greatest minds is something every single one of us has access to. When we can know what to look out for, we can refine it.

To spot your intuition, look at the times in your life when you knew something without a logical reason to come to that conclusion. Often, we can look back at when we didn't follow our intuition as an example of when it was trying to communicate with us. It can be difficult to go with our gut in a society that conditions us to believe that hunches are unreasonable. Yet, hunches inform a lot of our behavior without us entirely realizing, and its usefulness is undeniable. Intuition is the gift of discernment. We use discernment every day, from gauging how we feel to deciding what we're going to do. The artist uses discernment with every brushstroke. The surgeon must discern every swipe of the scalpel. Intuition doesn't contradict logic, it works through whatever mental structures we create and nurture. The more you know logically and informationally, the more intuition can help guide your approach in everything you do.

We must get out of our own way and actively strive to decondition the things that prevent us from recognizing our spiritual nature. When we do our part, the Universe has a way of doing its part, sometimes in the most mysterious of ways.

As a medium, I've seen a lot of mind-blowing validations through readings. However, the most mystical thing I've ever experienced didn't happen when I was doing a reading. It happened while I was fixing a printer.

In 2016 I lived in an apartment with my then-boyfriend and parents. One Sunday morning, the printer in my room malfunctioned and I asked my mom to help me undo the jam. She obliged, and we worked on fixing it on my bedroom floor for about fifteen minutes. I was becoming increasingly frustrated, but then, out of nowhere, it happened. Suddenly the printer I was staring at intensely lit up as if someone was shining a flashlight directly on it. From behind me, a light source was illuminating the room within seconds. A bizarre buzzing noise radiated through the entire room and made my hair stand on edge. My mom and I looked at each other, and then turned around to see the source of the light. Only about six feet away near the ceiling was a moving light source, bright blue in color. It measured about three feet wide and three feet long, and I've never seen anything like it. We were stunned. We both watched as this light source near the ceiling began to gradually change. The bright, sky-blue light that electrified the room began appearing to collapse on itself, and as this happened it was encircled in a yellow light that floated like a mist. From this mist, golden embers of light fell to the ground onto the carpet below. It lasted no more than a few moments; we watched as this light seemed to collapse under its own weight. When I saw the golden embers begin falling to the ground, I leapt underneath it and tried to grab any residue that fell on the floor. My efforts were in vain. As I grasped at the light with my mom beside me, my then-boyfriend walked into the room and his jaw dropped. All three of us were witnessing the single most bizarre experience any one of us had ever witnessed, and probably ever will. After only a few seconds, the light collapsed entirely and disappeared, the static noise no longer more than a fleeting buzz.

None of us could make any sense of the experience. We took into consideration everything from ball lightning to an electrical malfunction, but none of us could even begin to understand the profound effect the light had on all of our lives. We didn't talk about it to the extent that you'd expect; it was a deeply personal experience that impacted us all in different ways. My mom has a hard time discussing it and acknowledges that it was the oddest thing to ever occur to her. My then-boyfriend and I still stay in touch, and I recently asked him about the light. Surprisingly, he said that the sound was what initially stunned him, even before he walked in. The whole apartment seemed to radiate with a noise that he heard in the living room, which prompted him to come into the bedroom where he witnessed the light. The fact that there was no residue from the golden embers left me frustrated and confused. The beads of light that fell from the original source were about the size of a halved dollar bill, and yet they left no remnants or burns on the carpet. Whatever we witnessed that Sunday morning in a small apartment in LA originated from somewhere else. Of that I am certain.

My own experience fit the definition of a mystical experience: it was hard to describe or speak about for an abnormal amount of time. It sent me down a path of wanting to understand what it was and why it appeared in front of three people. It was short, but it was the most overwhelming experience of my life. I won't say that it felt like the presence of God, but there was an indescribable feeling of sentience to the light. It seemed like someone was in the room with me. This forever changed my views on the unknown, and if it hadn't been witnessed by two other sets of eyeballs, I wouldn't have believed my eyes.

Long before the experience with the light in the apartment, I had had moments of subtle strangeness that seemed to guide my life. I'd often dream of something, only to watch the same scene pan out the next day. I'd notice certain coincidences that seemed to emphasize aspects of things that I benefited from understanding. There were moments when the Universe intervened to send a message, and it was obvious. These moments of affirmation are what I call "Moments of Grace," and they've happened at pivotal times when I was willing to listen.

One of the earliest examples occurred when I was a teenager. I received a psychic reading of my own from a woman who walked into the shop where I worked. She asked me my birthday and without skipping a beat started relaying intimate information about me. I was stunned. She rattled off details about my childhood and told me things about myself that left me speechless. She knew my past, but even more interestingly, she started talking about my future. In her rapid-fire pace she predicted that when I was nineteen, I would receive life-changing news on the side of a mountain.

Years passed, and when I was eighteen I'd been in discussions with various television networks and had proven myself as a medium to countless executives and their friends and families. With the psychic's message still in my mind, I wondered if she had seen my developing career before I did. After multiple successful meetings, I was set to receive the news that a show I would star in was picked up by ABC Family, and I wondered if the psychic's message was simply off by a year. I was in such a hurry to get my career rolling, maybe the prediction got moved up!

But it wasn't meant to be. In the midst of the deal being finalized, I received news I wasn't expecting: the network was pulling out and had found a medium that fit their audience demographic more, and that was that. One day you're the cock of the walk, the next day a feather duster.

Despite my disappointment, I knew there had to be something around the corner. The psychic was uncannily accurate about so many things, and I was chomping at the bit to receive whatever news was in store.

Shortly after my nineteenth birthday, I was coming home from a long day of doing readings in Hollywood Hills. The cell reception is notoriously terrible in Hollywood Hills and when my mom's phone rang,

I figured I'd let it ring until we were out of the dead zone. Yet for some reason, my mom jerked the car to the side of the road and answered the call. The voice on the other end was my manager, Michael Corbett, and through the static I could make out only a few important words: "... *The E! network wants to do a show with you ... they greenlit your series!*" I was stunned.

We had met with E! prior to ABC Family, but it didn't pan out. It took rejection by one network to gain interest from the other. Never had I so evidently seen an example of one door opening when another is closed. As I processed what I was hearing on the phone, I looked up and realized where I was: sitting in my car on the side of a mountain that overlooked the Hollywood sign. At nineteen years old, I received the news that would change my life, and the sign was crystal clear.

2

Check Your Ego

The Great Saboteur

Our ego is our beliefs about ourselves. It's an identity of our own creation and conditioning, but it doesn't reflect who we truly are as souls. We think of our talents, abilities, and personalities as who we are, but these are all capabilities we have, not the defining features of our soul.

—*Tyler Henry,* Between Two Worlds: Lessons from the Other Side

One of my earliest memories provides a glaring insight into ego. When I was around five years old, a family friend was watching me, and we ran an errand. I wanted to make sure we'd be home in time for my mom to pick me up. I didn't want to leave my mom waiting for us, in case she had things to do. So, I asked my babysitter when we'd be going back home. She was in a bad mood and retorted that we'd go back home when she said so.

This only fired me up more, and I insisted that she

tell me when we'd be returning. "I'm the adult, you're the child, don't ask questions!" she hollered.

Without skipping a beat, I looked at her from the backseat and asked sternly, "Who are you to tell me what to do with my life?"

Therein began my lifelong reputation for asking thought-provoking questions. Though I was so young, part of me knew that my will was being denied, and my ego was pushing back. Already, at a young age, I'd created a defense system of asking questions and not taking no for an answer. This didn't always serve me, but it was the case. It's no wonder my mom adopted the saying, "If he's old enough to ask, he's old enough to know."

Man's oldest battles has been with himself. Carl Jung eloquently suggested that everyone has two sides: the self and the persona. The self is who you truly are, or as I call it, your soul. Your persona is the version of yourself you present to the world around you. When your self and your persona are too different, life becomes disharmonious. We all act differently in different environments, but the self follows us through every moment, quietly watching in the background as we socially shapeshift.

When you create space to be silent with yourself, it's easier to know your self. With no need for the defensive armor of the persona, solitude allows one to better know oneself. Some people have an extremely hard time being alone because it can force us to look deeper.

I believe that alone time is fundamental to spiritual growth. To truly know yourself, you must go inward and delve into the deep unconscious. Mystics throughout history went on a lone journey to find themselves, often into the wilderness or through a great distance. No matter what the fable, the mystic's journey involves a descent into solitude, and then an ascent back into society to share what they have learned from that place of introspection. Such is the path of the spiritual person.

When we face the world, our persona is wielded, and we present ourselves in the way our ego feels will be well-received. The persona is just a part of who we are, and yet most people go through their lives never separating themselves from what they present to others. From the moment we're born, how we define the world is shaped and molded by our experiences. It's like a bank: our life experience is deposited into our mental accounts and the extent that we withdraw wisdom is up to us. The conditioning of our ego forms the story we tell ourselves about everyone and everything, and oftentimes, it isn't painting the full picture.

The ego goes by many names and terms, but one of my favorites is "the inner saboteur." This phrase was popularized by RuPaul, who I read on *Hollywood Medium*. Because ego gets in the way of authenticity, it prevents us from executing our full potential. Therein lies the saboteur, always waiting to mold and change us based on the expectations imposed on it. From his perspective, being a drag queen was a way of mocking tightly held identity and breaking the societal expectations of traditional gender roles.

Not taking himself so seriously was a liberation from the seriousness of traditional identity.

The messages of forgiveness his departed father relayed exemplified the idea of accountability around the inner saboteur, an insidious system of habits and coping mechanisms that were only recognized after death. As is the case on the other side, hindsight is always 20/20.

Throughout his childhood, RuPaul's relationship with his father was strained and inconsistent. When his father was present, he often made promises to his young son that he never kept—emotionally abandoning and traumatizing him from a very early age. His father's ego ravaged his closest interpersonal relationships, wrecking his financial life as a result. He often found himself making choices that got in the way of his own happiness, which of course negatively impacted his son. RuPaul's father's message was clear: there was no longer denial, and no longer empty promises.

Despite his tumultuous home life, Ru's need for paternal support influenced him to be his own source of support. He had to be his own father figure. The damage his father's ego had on his family life made Ru aware of the importance of self-preservation and believing in yourself. He was determined to break the cycle of dysfunction.

Because RuPaul went into the reading experience

with a good dose of self-awareness (and years of therapy), he was able to understand the power in his father's message of personal accountability, recognize it, and forgive his dad in a way that hadn't been possible before. Through this message, he was able to appreciate his father in a way he was never able to when his dad was alive. He saw the good that came from the bad, and the resilience acquired through knowing oneself.

When we know better, we do better, and when his father let his ego go and shared his realizations, it inspired every living family member to understand and forgive—and helped their souls heal as a result. His father's life review was powerful! It enabled him to heal not only himself, but those he hurt along the way.

I tell Ru's story because identifying how our "ego" conditions us to respond to the world actually allows us to expose our inner saboteur. And when we can see how we get in our own way, we can then take a step back and get out of our own way. The more diligent we can be of our own behavior that doesn't ultimately serve us, the better off we are in the long run. We all do things that are against our best interests at times, and we must take note of when we see this self-destructive behavior playing out. It's an indication that our conditioning has taken our sights off the big picture and distracted us from our full potential.

We must remember that having a "big ego" means more than simply being self-absorbed, cocky, or narcissistic. These stereotypes represent only a small portion of how ego can affect us. Our self-esteem hurdles, life-style conditioning, and the internal beliefs we define ourselves by (for better or worse) all mold our ego. We often define ourselves by what we think, when we are really just the observer of our thoughts. When we implement this understanding into our lives, we can identify and improve upon our spiritual backseat driver.

My work acts as a constant reminder of ego. In a reading, I have to overcome my own ego in order to trust the process. If I'm too hung up on being perceived as right or wrong, valuable headspace is being taken up by self-imposed expectation. I mustn't be too confident, or too wary. Mediums are in a unique position in that, in order to do our job effectively, we have to be mindful of how ego skews our interpretations of messages. Mediums who are not actively on top of their egos tend to be megalomaniacs, and there's no shortage out there. We all look for external validation, but a medium's job revolves around it. We must perform feats perceived as supernatural, even if they're natural to us. No one can truly understand what we go through. We face harsh criticism and have to be self-assured and willing to trust our own narratives. This can get less-than-secure minds into trouble, and it is part of why I believe few famous mediums get along. True contentedness can be found in balance.

Every occupation requires decision-making, and it helps if we're confident in those decisions. Similarly, mediums have to have confidence in what information they bring forward. Everyone has to assert themselves sometimes, and we should strive to create an ego-structure that encourages us to make assertive, dependable decisions. That same structure should also keep us humble, willing to learn, and never too cocky.

This is a fine line that has to be navigated in my daily life. One example sticks with me as to how important it is to be assured, but not arrogant. I met with a woman for a reading during a press tour in NYC. As we filmed our reading, nothing seemed particularly out of the ordinary. Her mother had died a few years prior, and she made references to their final conversation. My client was elated with all of the validations that came through, and I was thrilled it was going to be shared with the world.

Then, it happened. The reading started winding down, but not before one final message. My client's departed mother needed her to know that she had a brother. I correctly intuited that my client had three known siblings, but her mother was insistent that there was a fourth. My client's entire demeanor changed, because this was not what she was expecting to hear. Everything in the reading had been spot-on up until this point, and the fact that it was so left field made my client question the validity of the other messages. I became frustrated, considering we'd just had a beautiful reading and she was letting one unidentified message get in the way of her own healing.

Ultimately, the filmed reading was scrapped. The

client didn't like that final message and felt uncomfortable broadcasting it to the world. All of my work was done, only to be deflated by a single mysterious message.

Nearly a year later, I received an email from the client. The bulk of her email was spent apologizing for shooting me down in our initial reading, because she discovered the message was correct. Shortly after we met, my client's father died. On his death bed, he admitted to his children that he had gotten a woman pregnant, and she had birthed a son. They had a sibling they never knew about.

My client had assumed the message meant that her mother had another child, not her father. The validity of the message was a resounding reminder of the power of spirits, and how important it is to honor their messages. It can be easy to blow off experiences or messages that don't fit our narratives, but we must be open-minded to reap the full rewards of these valuable moments. Though the reading never aired, it wasn't meant to. I was there to put the thought in the client's head, to introduce her to a truth that she'd later have to cope with under surprising circumstances.

People seeking out readings have a lot of expectations, and the nature of grief can make them focused on themselves. Sometimes, hard-headedness prevails, and I'm met with pushback. One such example happened a few years ago, when I was faced with an exceptionally difficult reading. The morning before, I was plagued with ominous feelings and was weirdly anxious. After doing over two hundred readings on the show, there were a lot of door knocks and gut drops. But this was different.

As I made my way up what felt like the longest driveway of my life, I knocked on the door. A million years passed, and then it opened. Standing there was a man dressed in chic layers, colorful eye makeup, and a large, obtrusive hat. It was Boy George.

He didn't go out of his way to be friendly, but he was polite enough. His reading was intense, with a number of departed friends wanting to be acknowledged. Yet no matter what I brought forward, it was shot down. Even the more nondescript impressions were denied, and it was evident I could've intuited his social security number and he'd still not cooperate.

His manager joined the reading after what felt like hours of pulling teeth. He was sympathetic, and began validating a number of the things George refused to acknowledge. It was evident that there was a public persona to keep up, and that wasn't one that gets vulnerable. This was a situation I'd encountered a few times throughout filming four seasons of *Hollywood Medium*. Celebrities provided an incredible insight into ego, and how the self and persona interact. Very often clients withheld validating information they knew was true out of fear of how the public might respond to it. Everybody wants to be liked, but sometimes public figures I read on camera were selective in what they were willing to show about their personal lives.

My time with Boy George was, ironically, one of my

favorite moments on *Hollywood Medium*. It took about three seasons for me to feel that way, but it holds a special place in my heart. George was gracious enough to talk with my assistant Charlie after the reading, and I appreciated how kind he was to her. The steely-eyed, made-up character in front of me seemed almost inaccessible by design, and I wondered how he'd have responded if cameras weren't rolling. I gathered that, in some ways, his costume was his armor, and his appearance was a way of controlling what people saw when they looked at him.

This reading made me face my own ego and accept the possibility of being perceived as inaccurate. Through being faced with the ego of a client, I had an insight into my ego and what I could do better next time around. This exemplifies an opportunity we all have when we're upset: to look at people as mirrors into ourselves.

How we present ourselves to the world shows how we want to be perceived. The picture we paint of ourselves for the world says a lot about how we view ourselves, and this can provide valuable insight into the universal human condition. Within everybody exists a child that just wants to be validated, and our ego is left to do what it will to compensate for that fact.

When we're in a confrontational situation, it's easy to want to go on the offense, but it's important to hear out opposition and assess if there is any truth that we can benefit from, despite the sore source. All too often people don't actually listen to what's riling them up. In the words of Mark Twain, "If we are supposed to talk more than we listen, we would have two tongues and one ear."

That said, no one likes to be criticized. It's painful to be misunderstood or intentionally taken the wrong way. As a boy, I watched how critics trashed psychics like Sylvia Browne and John Edward on the internet, and I felt horrible for them. I knew that if I were to step into the role of a medium in the public, those same critics would come after me.

They have. They come to my live shows and heckle my appearances and insult how I look or my sexuality when they can't find anything arguable in a reading. Just recently, a man stole a backstage pass and walked into my dressing room, cornering me before a live show. I've received credible death threats, which are always reported to the police.

I've said it before and I'll say it again: there's a difference between being skeptical and being cynical. Skepticism is an important virtue, and it leads to better understanding. But cynicism is a trait that's been romanticized and conflated with intelligence. It is not. Cynics have their mind made up regardless of what a reading shows, no matter how profound. They use confirmation bias to validate their vitriol when they can, and do mental gymnastics to accuse all mediums of being deceptive. Scientism masquerading as healthy skepticism is regressive. If science can't quantify it right now, then proponents of scientism say it doesn't exist. Yet they ignore the fact that there were countless times in history where we hadn't yet made a discovery because of technological, scientific, or quantifiable limitations.

The continual prevalence of mediums shows that Spiritualism is alive and well. People are comfortable discussing the subject now more than ever in history. With every notable medium that emerges, there are a thousand critics chasing their coattails with the goal of aligning their name with an upcoming celebrity.

We all have to deal with naysayers at one point or another, and it's important to know the truth of who you are. When you're affirmed in who you are and what you represent, you'll be unwavering in your strength. We all have soft spots, triggers, and sensitive topics, but when you know yourself and accept yourself, you create a foundation that can't be overthrown.

Sometimes, people's spiritual beliefs actually impede their receptivity to a reading, and it's an insight into how our beliefs can get in our own way. Some of the loveliest clients I've had were religious, and it often took a lot of explaining to get them on the same page with me. Growing up in a Presbyterian household, I was well aware that many Christian denominations disliked mediums, referring to them as necromancers. A video on this very subject was played at a church youth group meeting I attended, and I walked out and never returned.

A prayer circle was held at a church for my soul by a concerned parent in my hometown. People judge what they do not understand, and we must recognize our own calls to judgement. The moments where we're called to judge other people may reflect qualities we don't like in ourselves, and we can learn from other people's examples without getting riled up.

I never understood how medium abilities contradicted religious belief. Jesus, and in some belief systems the saints, all performed miraculous feats that verified God's existence. How is being a medium any different when it's applied in a way that's healing and productive?

One funny anecdote happened during my reading with Kenya Moore. She was nearly nine months pregnant and was legitimately kind. Yet, every time we talked about departed loved ones, she seemed uncomfortable and stoic. When a departed mother figure for her acknowledged the upcoming birth of her baby, a diaper bag flew off the shelf from behind her. I would have found this to be an extremely comforting sign, but she seemed uneasy. I later understood that she came from a very religious background, and I couldn't help but wonder if that was why there may have been some hesitance to connect with the next realm. What some would find comforting, others find frightening. Regardless, she was genuine and lovely, and I felt that it was a privilege to be able to sit with her at such a transformative time in her life.

A good rule of thumb is that if your spirituality invokes continual fear, it might not be the most productive belief system you could be adopting. We're all entitled to our own beliefs, but our beliefs should liberate us, not ensnare us. Any belief system rooted in dogma and persecution only leads to repression and complexes. People are what they are, and we have to be willing to set aside labels for what we don't understand. It's easy to jump to insidious assumptions around things we don't "get," but applying a little inquisitiveness will get you further than any judgement ever will.

Another time where religion factored into a reading occurred when I met with Melissa Joan Hart. She was incredibly down to earth despite being a little apprehensive to be read by a medium. Regardless, I was glad she let me know from the get-go, and it gave me a valuable opportunity to share my take on the subject. To truly understand the Bible, I think it's important to take into account both historical and contextual factors. Mediums of the Biblical age were considered archaic and barbaric in their beliefs. Spiritual communication was vilified and deemed Pagan, while speaking with a personal god through prayer was considered fine and dandy. It's only a sin when God talks back!

Once Melissa was able to contextualize the experience into the framework of her belief system, we had an incredible time. She was one of the best readings ever done on the show, and we've stayed in touch since.

Of all of the readings done on my show, my time with Alan Thicke was unlike any other. To this day I get emotional when I think about him, because of how loved he was and how much I wish I could have saved him. We met nearly three months before he died suddenly of a heart condition. In our reading, a loved one came through that had died of the same heart condition, and explicitly told him to get his heart checked. I went on for longer than normal about how important this message felt, and emphasized it to an annoying extent. In his iconic fatherly tone, he responded only with, "Thanks, Dr. Tyler!"

Alan was a lighthearted, funny man who didn't want to go too deep. He didn't strike me as a big believer in mediums, and responded to my messages with zingers and jokes. He certainly appreciated the experience, but humor was just how he coped with talking about personal things publicly. I wondered if that aspect of his ego may have prevented him from understanding the seriousness of the message I relayed. In this way, ego can unintentionally get in our way, even if our intentions are good.

It was clear in our reading that the reading was more for his wife than for him, and Tanya and I became close friends through the experience. Her love for Alan was so evident in everything she did, and I did a follow-up reading with her after he passed. The day of our follow-up reading, I had no idea how she'd be.

Before I arrived to meet her, I'd been repeatedly having visions of eggs, sunny-side up. Then, those visions were followed up with a sun rising. I had no clue what it meant, but it certainly wasn't because I was hungry for breakfast.

When I met with Tanya that day, it was one of the first things I mentioned. She was stunned. She acknowledged that the moment she received the news of Alan's death, she said out loud, "The sun will never come out again."

Through two very simple images, Alan conveyed from the other side that her sun would indeed rise again, and life would get better. His connection to her from the other side was a validation of the love they shared, and that until they're reunited again someday, he'll be with her every day of her life.

Not only has working with celebrities for extended periods of time given me an insight into ego, but doing press has also taught me valuable lessons. For movie stars and singers, going on press tours is often the most boring and mundane part of the creative process. When you're a medium, however, being interviewed can go a million different directions. I never know whether the interviewer is supportive or detractive. I never know how a piece will be edited, or through what angle it will be presented in its final form. As a result, I have to surrender to the process and be secure in who I am, no matter what I'm faced with. One of the most bizarre interactions I've ever had with the press happened before my interview on *Larry King Live*.

The entire experience was like a fever dream. Where the show is filmed is a pretty cramped space with huge stained-glass window–looking lights that make the set feel like you're about to confess your sins in interview form. I was reassured when I found out that a former client of mine, Moby, was the interview before me. Excellent! A familiar face, I thought. Moby finished up his interview, came into the lobby, and was gracious as always. I wanted to talk to him more, but nature was calling, and I had to run to the restroom.

As I walked down the tight quarters into the only bathroom on set, I swung open the door and was met by a figure, very much in the process of using the facilities. I squinted, and then recoiled, realizing it was Larry King in the flesh. Talk about an introduction!

I screamed, Larry King screamed, and I was mortified. Then, within seconds of him exalting, "You're supposed to be psychic, didn't you know I was in there?!" cameras were rolling and it was time to do our interview. We were clearly off to a great start.

Larry was a balanced interviewer, but skilled at making you comfortable only to hit you with a left-field question. As we went back and forth, he made many comments that I could've taken as insulting. He seemed baffled at the suggestion that all departed people ultimately achieve peace in the hereafter, and was insistent that couldn't be. It was clear Larry wasn't very well-versed in the idea of spiritual transformation after death, so when he followed that up with a surprisingly philosophical question, I responded, "Good question."

Well, he didn't like that very much. He's Larry King. All of his questions are good questions, to him. I didn't let it faze me. He proceeded to joke about my name and implied a lack of trustworthiness around people with two first names. I had to hold back from asking him if he'd say the same thing about Ray Charles.

All in all, our time together was a test of my ego. There were times when I was frustrated that he seemed to make minimal effort in understanding, and in his famous Larry King way, he often talked over me before I could formulate a coherent thought. From beginning to end it was a surreal experience, and one I'll forever be grateful for. Other than listing popcorn as my guilty pleasure, I did a pretty good job at standing my ground. I was thankful to share time with the iconic journalist . . . and what an introduction!

Everybody wants to be validated, but not everyone is validating. As the saying goes, you can be the biggest, juiciest peach in the world, and there's still going to be people who hate peaches. Being true to who we are requires courage. Being authentic puts our neck on the line, but it's the only way worth being. Courage can only rise to the occasion when fear is present. We must all do our part to live in alignment with who we are and what we stand for. No matter the opposition we face, through every hurdle there is an opportunity to learn, internalize, and grow.

This is made immensely clearer when people die. As mentioned earlier, there's a process which every single one of us will go through when our time comes. This process involves consciously witnessing every life event we've experienced. Not only that, but we gain an understanding of how other individuals were changed by our presence in their lives. This ripple-effect understanding gives our consciousness insight into the true feelings of other people and what informed their behavior. This process, I believe, is the result of an expansion process that happens to our consciousness when we pass on. We don't know everything when we die, but we know a lot more than we did before.

The life review is pivotal in reaching peace. It might not sound pleasant to re-watch everything you've ever gone through, but you experience it in a less human way. The consciousness, separate from its body, rapidly begins processing its ego upon death. We recognize the shortcomings of others and are made immensely clear about our own dysfunction. More significantly, we begin to understand why we did what we did, and why certain setbacks happened to us.

This process is introspective. Even the most sociopathic individuals are forced to understand the magnitude of the pain they caused. Ultimately, we realize our existential place in the universe, and we "get" why we were here. It's as if the puzzle pieces fall into place. When we've realized how our one consciousness changed everyone it ever came into contact with, we become enlightened as to the roles we and others played.

When I conduct a medium reading, souls that come through may be at varying stages in their ego death process. It's made clear to me that linear time does not exist in the next realm, so a life review isn't like a movie in rapid succession. It's a process, but not one that necessarily abides by a traditional beginning, middle, and end. It's described to me as being able to have multiple experiences at once.

Imagine you're on a street in Los Angeles. From this street perspective, you only have an awareness of one road. If we were to put you on a satellite high over Los Angeles, however, you'd be able to see many roads. By changing your distance, you're able to observe more, and watch many things unfold in many different places, all at once.

This is what the life review process is like. It's the most insightful experience a human can go through, and it can be likened to a birth in and of itself. Through a process of acceptance and resolution, we're born into the next realm purified of our Earthly turmoil. We ultimately retain all the lessons our life experience taught us, and move onto the next state of existence. No good deed goes unseen, nor does any malicious intention. All is brought to light in the grand experience of a life review.

By recognizing what informed our behavior and the behavior of others, we strip away the crutches we leaned on to exist on planet Earth. We don't need them anymore. Social pressures, coping mechanisms, and imposed expectations are all put to rest. In many ways, when we die, part of us does meet an end, and that part is ego. The stripping of these existential layers is fundamental to the rebirth process and equips us with the tools we need to navigate the next realm. Like a butterfly emerging from a cocoon, our soul and newfound perspective aren't concerned about the happenings of their former caterpillar self.

Recently, I was discussing ego death with a longtime friend. I explained to him my thoughts on the matter, and how we could all benefit from taking a long, hard look at our ego. He said that he had heard of the concept after he experimented with psilocybin mushrooms. He felt like it was helping him make spiritual progress by helping him reach ego death while he was still alive. I didn't want to come off as judgmental, but I felt that equating hallucinations to spiritual visions demeaned the significance of truly mystical experiences. Furthermore, aiming for ego death while you still have human responsibilities is counterintuitive. No one should try to kill off their ego, as that's just repressing something that can't be destroyed.

There are entire groups of people that use ayahuasca to reach spiritual states, particularly in the Amazon, but that's done ceremonially. The religious aspect to that practice can absolutely inspire personal growth. Kicking back on your couch and ingesting a hallucinogen, however, is not the same as having a ritualistic spiritual revelation. Furthermore, these substances can make people unstable and out of touch. Our body truly is our temple, and we should treat spirituality as a path with no shortcuts. We shouldn't aim to destroy our ego; we should strive to reconstruct it and view it as a work in progress.

Obviously, we can't experience a life review when we're still alive. However, we can review how we live. My understanding of the life review process has made me more aware that people provide valuable insights into ourselves. We're all capable of the same things, both productive and destructive, and what we do with our power comes back to face us when we die.

I don't believe in a judgmental God. I believe that the universal fabric of existence revolves around growth. As our consciousness continues, new information is acquired. New insight is gleaned. The nature of eternal consciousness means that we take our experiences with us, and they leave an imprint on the world around us. We're left to assess ourselves and come to terms with how we lived and died. For this reason, I try to be mindful of the way I conduct my life. I try to reverse engineer aspects of the life review process by trying to put myself in others' shoes. I try to look at the consequences of my actions, both intentional and unintentional. This mindfulness has shown me the importance of accountability, and I always strive to do better.

If our ego is defined as the filter we see ourselves and others through, then narratives are defined as the stories we tell ourselves about what we see. Like a narrator who reads a story, our inner narratives inform how we perceive the world and ourselves. What we tell ourselves has extreme power over us. How we frame a situation determines its seriousness to us. Inner narratives are important tools for discernment that we need in order to survive, notice patterns, and come to conclusions. Narratives aren't implicitly problematic; we need them. What becomes an issue is when our ego misinforms our narratives, and our perspective becomes wonky. When this is repeated throughout a lifetime, going unchecked, people can end up having some pretty skewed perceptions of the world and themselves. Thus, it's important to be mindful of what you tell yourself. Technically, spirits can have narratives. They can convey their understandings of things, and therefore, they have a narrative. If ego is processed, however, these narratives aren't hindered by our human perspective. This is why souls often realize things that they didn't know when they were alive. Spirits come through with different degrees of ego death. Some seem to be incredibly self-aware and almost enlightened, while other spirits seem to still be very much processing their lives and deaths. Considering this process isn't limited to linear time, spirits may all be at different levels of shedding their former incarnation.

This has inspired me to want to do as much work as possible while I'm here to deconstruct unhealthy narratives. When we're upset, it's easy to react. Yet it's imperative that we get to a place where we can become the observer of our thoughts, not defined by them. Reactions often come directly from our ego. If we can observe outside of how we'd like to react for a moment, our feelings often change. How often have you said something reactionary, only to regret it moments later? Any time you felt the need to put your foot in your mouth, ego got you in trouble.

Responding, not reacting, is an important distinction. In the Buddhist belief system, words are sacred. Only speaking when you truly have something to say will make people listen to you a lot more. When we put thought into the words we wield, we realize their power over ourselves and others. Going through life reacting to everything, and by default being thrown into imbalance, is exhausting. Mindfulness is efficiency. It's a way to get the most, and make the most, of every moment.

When we're quiet, we can hear the whispers of our intuition. Reducing the power of our ego on our consciousness makes intuition a lot easier to notice. By being the observer of your thoughts, you begin to realize your true nature. Every thought you have, every belief you hold, are all streams of input that you either accept or reject. Distinguishing yourself from your thoughts is a major step in living more meaningfully.

As a toddler, I'd take everything out of the refrigerator and line up everything of a corresponding color. As I grew older, this anxious compulsive behavior manifested through counting, turning light switches on and off, and a number of irritating compulsions.

For years I struggled nightly with wondering if every door was really locked, even after I'd checked multiple times. Every time I said goodbye to my parents, I would have the intrusive thought that it may be the last time we ever see each other. If anything, the nature of the condition has given me opportunities to apply what I know, and mindfulness has single-handedly been the best tool to separate anxious thoughts from true intuitions. As a child, the condition caused me a lot of anxiety, but it has made me a more mindful adult.

When the departed come through, they often recognize that aspects of mental health played into their beliefs and behavior. Since consciousness continues and is purged of its former structures, those who struggled with mental illness acknowledge a change in perspective. People in the grips of addiction come through without addictive qualities. Individuals who are taunted by their biochemistry in life generally find peace when they pass away. Even the most mentally unwell of people come through with an understanding of how important their lives were, and how important the human experience is. Those who end their lives intentionally often realize what informed that decision, and how life could have been better if they stuck around. The life review process gives us understandings of others and ourselves, and how we all influence the collective experience. Not only do we come to understand the far-reaching impact of our actions, but we understand how others changed us in ways our ego prevented us from seeing in life. We are able to perceive what could have been, what was, and what it means in the present moment. Life reviews are a pivotal time in a soul's existence, where our understandings and definitions of life and purpose are called into question, and evolve.

It's important that we do everything we can to stay alive, and learn everything we possibly can. No matter what we go through, we must strive to do better, evolve, and establish a balanced foundation. Our ego tells us all sorts of things, and oftentimes we wouldn't speak to our friends the way we speak to ourselves. Separate your thoughts from who you are, and you'll be a much happier observer.

We live in a triggering world. When we think of the word trigger, we think of something that sets into action a series of other things. It's comparative to a bullet leaving a barrel or a line of dominoes gaining momentum and falling in rapid succession. Mental triggers have this effect on our ego. They set us off.

Mental triggers are part of the human condition. They're those things that get brought up in conversations and make you recoil internally, wishing the subject could be dropped altogether. I think you'd be hard pressed to find a human being alive today that hasn't dealt with some kind of trauma, and trauma often influences what triggers us. The negative emotions behind triggering topics and situations can make us avoidant, and drastically alter the scope of our living.

Because sadness, shame, and anger are such powerful emotions, they shape and inform our behavior. They're all emotions none of us want to feel, but they're inevitable from time to time. We should make an effort to understand our shadow, and what invokes feelings of anxiety. They can teach us something. Since we can't undo traumatic events, the only control we have is what we do with it. The more acceptance we can establish over that which we cannot control, the closer to contentedness we'll be. While that's easier said than done, it's a pragmatic approach to peace. By knowing what we can't control, we can put more energy into what we can. Again, living mindfully is an efficient way of living.

This topic was exemplified in my filmed reading with Wendi McLendon-Covey. Her reading was incredibly emotional, as we connected with a departed uncle figure whose life was as tragic as his death. As I communicated with him, I determined that he had been gone for a long time and had died at an early age. He conveyed to me that he lived his life in a perpetual state of triggers, never truly finding peace with who he was. He was gay. At a time when LGBTQ people couldn't be who they were, he was forced into the closet and died by his own hand as a result.

Living was unbearable, and he no longer saw the point. Because he couldn't be true to who he was, he felt disassociated from his purpose and fulfillment. Shame molded his personality, and having to maintain secrets only developed into more evasive behavior. He needed someone who could help him and let him know it was okay to be who he truly was. Yet, no one could meet the real man, or at least what he was hiding. By having this elephant on his back, he wasn't able to live authentically. Interestingly, a poem by Shel Silverstein called "The Mask" came to mind. The poem focuses on two individuals who have blue skin and try to hide that fact from one another. It ends with:

> They searched for blue,
> Their whole life through,
> Then passed right by—
> And never knew.
>
> —SHEL SILVERSTEIN

We can only live authentically when we notice our triggers and overcome them. We all share in the human experience, and you're not the first person to be in the bind you're in, no matter what it may be. Someone, somewhere, can relate to what you're going through. When we can be honest about who we are, we put forward our best face. Wendi's loved one found peace in the hereafter despite the fact that it evaded him in life. He was able to see how the influence of others changed how he viewed himself. He realized through his life review that he was the victim in the situation, and that nothing was truly wrong with him. All the shame he felt was a condition of society, and he fell victim to those pressures. His soul couldn't undo his actions, but he understood what informed them. This ultimately led to acceptance and, through this acceptance, peace. He realized through his life review process how many people really were there for him, even if he couldn't see it at the time. He saw how different choices would have led to different results. He seemed taken aback by the support that quietly existed, that he never realized because of shame. Through his journey of self-realization, he saw how societal pressure warped his ego, hijacked his narratives, and made him feel terrible about himself. How we frame the hardest of circumstances heavily defines the power they hold over us. Living authentically means that we're free, no longer having to upkeep the undue expectations of others.

I had to come to terms with one of my biggest triggers recently, under the most bizarre set of circumstances I could imagine. It would set me down a path of self-discovery and make me look at how I identify myself. It involved a murderous old lady and a 23andMe genealogy test. For the first twenty-three years of my life, the woman I was told was my mom's mother was a mysterious figure in my life. She wasn't exactly in my life in a physical sense, because she had served thirty years in prison for the murder of two people. When my mother was twelve, the woman she called Mom was charged with shooting and killing two people and trying to cover it up. Not only that, but she made my mom's brother bury the bodies at a motel under the threat of death. Evidently the woman got wrapped up with the Mexican mob, which was particularly strange because she was a creole Native American who spoke French.

The secondhand shame that this woman created for my mom was immense, and my mom did everything she possibly could to not emulate her.

All I ever knew was that this woman was named "Stella," and the stories of her abuse rival some of the most horrible stories of child abuse I've ever heard. Stella was born in the bayou swamps of Louisiana in the 1930s, without a birth certificate, along with her thirteen brothers and sisters. Some of her brothers would grow up to become registered sex offenders. She spoke fluent French and partial English, and took my mom everywhere to act as an interpreter, reading signs and giving driving directions.

When my grandmother was arrested when my mom was twelve, a prayer was answered. My mom went on to get adopted by her school secretary and janitor (who happened to be married), and they gave her a loving home. Stella's story was so sensational that people knew of my mom's situation and remembered it even as the years passed.

As I got older and understood the magnitude of her actions, I became ashamed of Stella. A cousin of mine went to the same school as me, and the sensational story about our mutual grandmother was spread around school. Kids made fun of me, and I could understand the shame my mom carried with her for most of her life. The dark cloud of her actions carried through generations, and it had a deeply detrimental effect on my life during childhood. Countless times I'd look at my mom and ask, "Are you sure she's really your mother?"

My mom is the kindest human being I've ever met. She epitomizes what it means to be a diligent, loving mother. Those who know my mother, love her. Her eyes light up when she smiles that comes from such an authentic place of goodness. She's everything my grandmother was not. I couldn't understand how I could have Stella's blood running through my veins, and it made me feel poorly when I thought about that fact.

Last year, I decided to get my mom a genealogy test for Christmas. I was feeling sentimental and was curious to learn more about the Native American side of my mom's family. She did the swab, sent it in, and the results came in. She was predominantly Italian. That was weird, we thought. Surely it was my mom's father's side that must have unknowingly had an Italy connection. We didn't think much of it, and moved on.

Fast forward a few months later, my mom and I arrived at LAX after a long series of live shows across the country. We were exhausted from the six-hour flight, and when we got in the car, I was ready to doze off. But then her phone rang. For some reason, I was jolted alert. Something on a deep, visceral level stirred inside me, and I had no control over what I was feeling. It was like someone threw ice water on my head.

"Hello?" she said.

Things got quiet for a moment, and she listened. I

heard only vaguely a man's voice on the other end with a strong Southern accent. A few moments passed, and then my mom's face changed. Complete and total shock set in. After asking who the man was, she learned that he had found my mom's number online. He had done a genealogy test for his mother, and he was calling her to tell her that he found her long-lost half sister.

My mom assumed her father must have gotten someone pregnant and that was what this phone call was about. That came to a screeching halt when the man said that he determined through his research that their relation could only be through his mother's mother. That meant that this man, who was supposedly my cousin, was saying that Stella wasn't my grandmother.

We were stunned. My mom went silent, processing the implications of the phone call. We considered that it could have been a prank, but he sent us his mother's DNA chart to show the similarities. An actual DNA test was ordered, and a few weeks later it was confirmed that my mother had an entire family that was desperately searching for her. This also meant that Stella had knowingly kidnapped my mom, and never revealed to my mom that she wasn't really her daughter.

I was enraged. Stella, now in her eighties and out of prison, was even more menacing than I thought. As the story unfolded, it was revealed that my mother was obtained illegally as a baby, and her birth certificate forged. She did not know if her birthday was really February 14, or if her given name was really even

Theresa. My biological grandmother would spend the rest of her life looking for my mom, crying herself to sleep at night because her little girl was missing. My actual grandmother's name was Mary, and she was said to be a jolly, kindhearted person who dealt with some difficult things. She was left to raise three children alone and wasn't able to keep my mom without putting financial strain on everybody. She spent her whole life looking for my mom, hoping someone could find her adult daughter and they could be reunited. She died in 2003 of Alzheimer's, never getting to see through her wish. My newfound family told us that Mary, even in the depths of dementia, remembered the daughter she could never find. She cried for her, even as an old woman, remembering her little girl.

My mom would later go on to put a face to the voice on the phone. My cousin Nick along with his mother Mary, my uncle George, and a whole gamut of cousins had spent a lifetime looking for us. My aunt said that my grandmother and aunt would often watch television and wonder if my mom might be one of the newscasters. They looked for visual similarities from people on television, which I think may have been both intuitive and an indication of how desperate they were to find her.

Now reunited with a family she didn't know she had, she wanted answers. I was incensed at Stella and wanted to understand how she could steal a child and lead me and my mom on for decades, thinking we were blood relatives. Apparently, my mom had the same questions, and after multiple attempts, she was able to get Stella on the phone.

Now frail and hoarse, Stella answered the phone, and my mom put it on speaker. I listened as this woman, the villain of my childhood and a dark cloud of shame in my family's life, engaged in small talk. My mom casually revealed that she learned that she was stolen as a baby, and Stella's tune changed. She was eerily coherent, and seemed to be able to read our intentions through the phone. When my mom asked for details about the circumstances of how she obtained her, Stella retorted, "Ask your son. He sees things. He'll know the truth."

I saw red. The trigger of my life was now taunting me through a phone call. All the humiliation Stella put both me and my mom through was inexcusable, and yet here she was, trying to humiliate me one last time. I don't know the truth, by the way, about every detail of my mother's childhood. It is impossible to not be biased about a situation that has been so traumatic. This makes getting a reading on the subject next to impossible. I'm too close to it, it's too painful, and my intuition is rendered useless in any endeavors to find the truth. There's an irony to it all, in the sense that the one time in my life my ability would have come in handy the most, I'm unable to use it.

No one knows the true circumstances by which Stella obtained my mom, and as I write this, I'm still coping from how jolting the situation was. Realizing Stella was not my grandmother exemplified how much her actions influenced how I felt about myself. I thought for so long that because we shared DNA, something might be wrong with me too. I was scared that whatever lurked in her, lurked in me.

And then, one day, it was all removed. If she hadn't engaged in her act of evil, Stella would be just a stranger to me. We have no more relation than anyone on the street. Her sins are not for me to carry. I didn't realize how much secondhand shame I held until it was swept away over the duration of a fifteen-minute phone call.

This experience was an intimate look at identity and made me realize how much we define ourselves in relation to other people. Whether it's meeting their expectations or taking on their actions as if they're our own, we are influenced by the people around us. We must be mindful to the extent that other people shape how we define ourselves. I didn't realize the burden I carried, until it was carried away.

As we've covered in this chapter, our ego drives our lives. There is no destroying it, only molding it to work for us. We're faced with choices every day that exemplify our relationship with our ego, and that's made apparent in the behavior of others. The ego is like a machine that pumps out our views on things, and it's made up of many moving parts. Our conditioning molds our ego into responding in certain ways, to preserve itself. This conditioning interacts with our triggers. Triggers act as massive red flags on what we need to look at, learn from, and try to accept.

Where we apply resistance is an indication of what we must be persistently mindful of. When we're faced with pushback, either internal or external, we must be willing to listen to what it has to teach us. The less we can take personally, the better. After all, everybody is only projecting what they feel to be true, based on the discernment of their own ego. This fact doesn't invalidate the true nature of situations, but it acts as a reminder that everybody has an opinion. Take it into consideration, and grow.

The departed learn a lot about the beliefs they hold when they die. Through the life review process, and ultimately ego death, peace is obtained. By implementing more acceptance into our lives, we can put to rest that which we cannot control. We can find acceptance through forgiveness, compassion, and the ability to truly see from someone else's perspective. All of these things are tools that can empower us to reframe our pain and control what we do with it. When we can forgive someone that has hurt us, we evict them from our headspace. View your mind as the sacred vessel it is: don't let people in it rent-free.

Fear is a self-preservation. It makes us want to do some things and avoid others. It can warp the reality of situations into a triggering series of anxieties. Knowing what you fear gives you some control over what scares you, and in a sense unmasks a lurking villain. Knowledge is power, and the more you make an effort to know yourself, the more you'll be able to better navigate the external world.

One of the most resounding messages that gets communicated to me from those who've lived and died is, "I should have just been kinder."

Those words stick with me in everything that I do, because in the end, it's all that truly matters. We have to be compassionate when it's hardest to be. We have to rise to the occasion when circumstance calls for kindness. We must kindle a light in the darkness of the world. This kindness should extend to ourselves, and we should apply forgiveness in liberal doses. We cannot stop others from being unkind, but we can be kind by not letting the harshities of others define how we view ourselves. We all have shortcomings, insecurities, and struggles, but therein lies a chance at growth. The decisions we make in this lifetime follow us into the next. Understanding the roles people play for others and themselves makes us a lot less judgmental.

When we understand our relationship with ego, our lives are transformed. When you become the observer of your thoughts and not defined by them, you break a paradigm of thought that has kept generations entrapped. So many people's actions are defined by an impulsive, reactionary mindset. Through introspection, you can transform your life through how you view it. In the end, our ego is a companion that we'll face and then depart from. In the meantime, we must nurture our relationship with it and create a balanced union.

3

Integrate Your Intuition
The Gift of Inner-Tuition

ntuition is something we all have, but seldom harness. We've all had moments where, in one way or another, something just didn't seem right. It can manifest as an off-putting first impression. Or, it gives us the idea to pick up the phone and call someone who happened to be thinking of us at that exact moment. It facilitates more than just fleeting, insightful moments. Intuition can act as an internal compass that never leads us astray. It can inform and transform our thoughts, behavior, and lives.

There're a lot of misconceptions about this primal part of our makeup. Validations of intuition aren't to be shrugged off. It's easy to go against our intuition and let our ego dictate our considerations. Intuition is more than just a one-off happenstance that is verified only after the incident occurs. It has served as an evolutionary perk for survival, but in recent times has become less relied upon than in our hunter-gatherer days. Still, intuition has moments where it shines through in our daily lives. Sometimes it's being able to empathize with someone's situation more than would logically make sense. We even apply intuition in our relationship with our pets. Think of when your family dog looks at you, and you just somehow know exactly what it wants. This inner-tuition is always on the back burner, separate from our ego but still very much a part of who we are.

Practically, intuition is instinct. The ability to intuit the intentions of potential predators has always served mankind. So, too, has the ability to find food and water. Intuition is a force that inspires breakthroughs. Just as it's a survival tool, it also guides us in new directions. It may have been responsible for moving us forward historically. Intuition may have been the glimmer of insight that inspired every hypothesis later proven to be true. Intuition acts as a stairway in which we cannot see the next step we're about to take, but we take it anyway. Intuition is a call that mankind has always answered, although it's often been attributed to God or not credited at all.

When refined, intuition can reveal enlightening truths about every aspect of our lives. It can strengthen our relationships and show us our strengths and weaknesses. A by-product of introspection is awareness. It can help us make more efficient and effective decisions in times of high stress. In business, going with our gut can aid in assessing who is trustworthy, and therefore who is worth working with. It expedites productivity and enhances every aspect of the human experience. In the spectrum of health, intuition can give us an insight into our overall well-being through introspection and self-analysis. Living mindfully and living intuitively go hand in hand. By creating an intuitive foundation, you can build a life of clarity and assurance.

Intuition moves us forward individually and collectively. It very rarely is felt for long intervals but more often in short, all-encompassing moments of clarity. Every epiphany, self-realization, and "aha!" moment starts first on an intuitive level. When we can listen to these whispers of guidance, it's made clear that we're not alone.

People often wonder if medium abilities and intuition are similar. In some ways, yes. Doing a reading requires me to enter into a state of mind where I'm able to notice the subtleties of whatever I may feel. When I know I'm on the right track with a particular validation, it feels like suddenly determining the answer to a math equation. Often, receiving messages from the departed feels like being imparted with memories that are not my own. It's always a fast process of transferring information, and in this way, medium readings are intuitive.

That said, we can still refine and practice our intuition without ever going down the medium path. In fact, I think there's very little we can do to "become" mediums. You either are or you aren't, and only so much can be done with what skills you have. Though I've grown through time in my communication skills, confidence, and delivery, my ability has always pretty much been the same. There's a line of thinking in the psychic community that everyone can become a medium, and I believe that exists purely to sell eager people psychic development courses. It's important to know what intuition is, and equally, what it isn't.

When we talk about living intuitively, it's really about unblocking the things that prevent your intuition from shining through. There's not one book, teacher, or resource that can make you an intuitive person. Familiarizing yourself with the concept is important, but only when it's put into practice is it practical. People like the idea of intuition; it's a novelty to most. Yet when intuition is made into a lifestyle, we become intensely more secure in our decisions. As a medium, I never feel alone in part due to all of the loved ones I connect with. Similarly, intuition is a friend that once you open the door for, you'll never want to leave.

In the following pages I'll be discussing the different ways intuition speaks to us, and how to noticeably see results with it. You'll develop a better understanding of how to tell the difference between intuition and anxiety. As we delve into the world of intuition, it's essential we not view it as the opposite of reasoning. Intuition informs reasoning. It's the groundwork for all the knowledge that moves us forward. With a little mindfulness and the tools to notice it, intuition will become a guiding force in your life.

As a medium, I have to be able to live intuitively. My job doesn't just start when I sit down to do a reading for someone; it begins the moment I wake up. I have to be aware from the moment I'm conscious of any potential blocks to my own intuition. Everybody has rough workdays, but if I have any form of confrontation in the morning, my whole day gets thrown off. Similarly, there can be physical blocks to my intuition, too. If I have a cold, I have a harder time noticing certain intuitive impressions because part of me is distracted. In a sense, to be a good medium, I have to maintain mental balance in order to do my job.

That sounds great on paper, but it isn't realistic. Life can be imbalanced sometimes. Anxiety and fear are just part of the path, and we have to honor those feelings, too. Not everybody can live intuitively 24/7. One of the most common questions I get is how to distinguish intuition from our own mental noise. Generally, we think of intuition as a "gut feeling." It creates a visceral reaction that's immediately brought to our attention. I think intuition is described too often as a feeling when it's actually a knowing.

Granted, you might have a strong emotional reaction to what your subconscious knows, but it's still originating as a knowingness. This is intuition. An anxious thought not rooted in intuition, however, has the power to completely send us down into our headspace and trigger a ripple effect of negative thinking. It might be directly tied to a previous trauma we've faced, making it all the more scary. This is anxiety.

Intuition is knowing, anxiety is feeling. Being that I have to be in an intuitive headspace for my work, I've been able to recognize the knowing nature of intuition, even when I have emotional reactions. Intuition communicates in quick flashes and catches us off guard. Anxiety comes to a head as a familiar fear and taps into our deepest concerns.

Intuition feels like some other source is giving you a nugget of knowledge. Many intuitives who do readings describe those nuggets as "downloads" of information. People have download moments all throughout their day, from intuiting which way to take to work, to knowing when the "right" time is to leave the house. All is intuition.

I did a reading with a woman who had an extraordinary and tragic story about intuition that demonstrates this distinction. She was a client of mine who I met with in my hometown one summer when I was a teenager. She booked a reading with me while she was in town because she was spending most of her time living in Turkey teaching abroad. I communicated with her departed son who had died in a car accident.

At the end of the reading, my client told me that an overwhelming knowingness came to her the moment her son died. He was killed in a vehicular accident while she was living in Turkey. She said that she was seated at her desk at work and looked up at the clock, noting the exact time. At the moment that she looked up, a flash of insight hit her. She knew her son had just passed. Then, tears filled her eyes and she wept. Shortly thereafter, she received the call from halfway around the world that her son had tragically died.

Being so far from her adult son, she worried about him in her day-to-day life. She had moments of anxiety where she wondered if he was okay, particularly when he wouldn't text her back right away. He always eventually did, like she knew deep down he always would. This was her anxiety. It was an uncomfortable thought that reoccurred throughout her time away from him.

The feeling, and more significantly, the knowingness, that came over her the moment her son died was unlike any anxious thought she had ever had before. It was more than a thought, she said. It was like a memory that hadn't happened yet.

That way of looking at intuition has always stuck with me. It's exactly how it feels. When I received my first premonition of my grandmother's death at ten years old, it felt like a memory that hadn't happened yet. I couldn't explain how I knew, but I knew. It was more than a feeling.

These examples demonstrate the importance of re-framing how we view intuition. It can seem stereotypical, like an alarming, irrational hunch that mothers sometimes get regarding their children's whereabouts, but that doesn't do intuition justice. Though mother's intuition is very real, we all have the ability to tap into this extremely powerful means of extrasensory perception.

One commonality that seems to exist around intuition is that it can be heightened after certain pivotal life events. Pregnancy, a significant loss, or a medical challenge are all known to send people down intuitive paths. I've had countless pregnant women reach out to me, saying that since their pregnancy they can't stop having prophetic dreams and feelings that are a lot more than hormones at work.

So, too, have people who've recently experienced a substantial loss. I fall into the category, as my grandmother's death acted as the catalyst for the emergence of my ability. One client of mine was plagued with intuitive moments after the passing of her mother. She and her mother would regularly listen to music together, and it was their "thing."

Shortly after her mother's death, she began having experiences that proved to be incredibly coincidental. She would be going about her day and then, out of nowhere, feel compelled to turn on the nearest radio. One time, this happened in her car. Another time, while she was on her phone in the middle of an email. The third time happened on her way to see me; she was in the car and felt compelled to change the channel to a specific one, at that specific time. In every one of these instances, the moment she turned the radio on, a significant song was playing that she and her mother shared.

The first time, it was a song that was played as she danced with her mother at her wedding. The second time it was a song her mother sang to her as a child. And the third time, as she drove to see me, the song that played at her mother's funeral was the exact song she unintentionally tuned into on the radio.

She couldn't exactly explain what led to these eerily profound moments; it just felt like something she had to do. She said that it was similar to knowing you left the stove on when you're halfway down your street. There was a sense of urgency behind the knowingness, and in her case, there wasn't even enough time to question it before it was put into action.

These moments were incredibly meaningful, and some may even take them as a message from her mother that she was still with her. But I believed something even more interesting was at play: my client was responsible for the action that brought forward the synchronicity every time. It was as if by following her intuition, she was receiving a message from her mother. Though my client was responsible for bringing the songs to her awareness through being compelled to change the channel, something was making her feel called to do this. That call would go on to happen many more times after our initial reading. With every time she felt compelled to put on a specific radio station, she was reminded of a specific memory with her mother. It was as if her mom was taking her down a trip through memory lane, one song at a time. My client was the unintentional DJ, and she found great comfort in this intuitive relationship with her mother's spirit.

Just as loss can act as a catalyst for inner knowledge, so can illness. Many historical figures dealt with poor health, only to receive visions thereafter. Abolitionist Harriet Tubman, who, as mentioned earlier, led slaves to freedom, falls into this category. As a young girl, she started having visions from God after a harrowing experience. When an irate slave owner hurled a lead weight at one of the other slaves, Harriet stepped in front of it. As she did, the weight struck her head and she fell to the ground. This would act as a catalyst for a lifelong series of narcoleptic fits and vivid visions of guidance. The synchronicity of her experience was immense. The brick was intended to hit someone else, and yet it hit her. If it hadn't happened, Harriet may not have as effectively navigated the underground railroad to the extent that she did. Her visions gave her guidance and reenforced her connection to a higher power. She trusted these visions from God at times when protection was needed most, and she listened to the whispers that led to freedom.

I recently experienced a medical intuition of my own when I foresaw something seriously wrong with my health. I had emergency brain surgery in 2014 after a mass was found near my brainstem. I knew that my brain was filling with fluid. I was later treated for hydrocephalus, or "water on the brain." I thought that would be the extent of my traumatizing health scares as a young adult.

Since that initial health scare, I was doing great. I began a multi-city live tour across the country, averaging around thirty-six cities a year. It's been a joy to be able to travel the country, share readings, and get to meet all of the lovely people that attend. I was particularly excited at the beginning of this year to travel up and down the West Coast for shows.

Fast forward to January 31, 2020. China was in the midst of the COVID-19 disaster, and Washington state would go on to be ground zero for the coronavirus epidemic less than a month later. I had just flown into Washington state the night before for two sold-out live shows with over 6,000 people.

I was in my hotel room doing my usual game-day rituals. I slept in, had a small meal, and enjoyed solitude. I spent the day meditating, and overall vegging out for the draining night ahead. I was lying in bed alone in the room when, out of nowhere, I was struck with a strange feeling, even by my standards.

It was more than a feeling. It felt like I was trying to remember something really important and couldn't focus on anything else. Assuming it was intuitive information coming through for all the readings I was set to do that night, I wasn't too concerned. That is, until I felt my chest collapse.

Out of nowhere, it was like someone turned on

a vacuum in my lung cavity. I knew then, without a shadow of a doubt, that my lung had spontaneously collapsed. I gasped for air and couldn't find breath to scream. I grabbed my phone, called my mom, and could only let out choking noises to let her know something was wrong.

She burst into the room shortly after, and we drove straight to the nearest hospital. By the time I was in the car on my way there, I was becoming increasingly dizzy and having a hard time staying conscious. When I got to the ER, a chest x-ray was done, and it was determined that I had suffered a 90 percent spontaneous pneumothorax. The x-ray showed my mangled lung, now like a deflated balloon, resting near my heart. Because of this, my heart rate was off the charts, and they needed to act immediately.

A chest tube was inserted between my ribs that went into my lung to help with breathing. Then there was emergency surgery to re-inflate my lung and stick it back up where it belonged. A surgery that was only supposed to be a few hours went on for nearly six. Evidently, the cause of my sudden illness was due to my genetics. I had pockets of flesh called bullae that were growing on my lungs, and one burst, causing a nearly total collapse.

I had multiple complications from surgery and was in the hospital for nearly three weeks. My lungs weren't healing as anticipated and required a chest tube the size of a hose. It was removed (while I was awake) after nearly a month in my lung cavity. It was an excruciating experience that couldn't have happened at a more synchronistic time. Considering that Kirkland, Washington, would go on to be one of the first hot spots for the coronavirus pandemic in the US, I had avoided a potentially deadly situation without even initially realizing it. More than that, if my lung hadn't collapsed the afternoon before my show, thousands of people would have joined together in close quarters, risking their lives.

It seemed that both my knowingness of my medical issue as it happened and the synchronicity of the timing were divinely sent. Again, a relationship between intuition and meaningful coincidence was made clear in a way that even I wasn't expecting. The timing of the experience seemed intentional, and lent me an opportunity to ultimately catch my breath. The experiences that initiate inner transformations can sometimes be scary, but they aren't accidental. Trusting the meaning in our experiences, even if we don't understand them at the time, can give us a renewed outlook as to why we experience them. Sometimes, they act as catalysts for great change.

Just as intuition can give us extra insight into the present moment, it can also give us glimpses into the future. I recently did a Skype reading with a woman whose loved one had died in a motorcycle accident. He communicated to me that he knew he was going to die shortly before he did. Apparently, he had told my client the morning before he died that, only the night before, he had dreamt of being flung from his motorcycle. While he wasn't the type to take this seriously, she was.

When it came time for him to come over to her house later in the day, she told him over the phone, "Don't take your motorcycle. I love you."

That would be her last conversation with him. On a familiar road that he'd traversed many times, his motorcycle mysteriously went off the road at a high speed, and he was killed instantly. His unwillingness to listen to what his intuition was clearly telling him led to his tragic demise. I suspect that the dream was never meant to save his life; its purpose was probably to give my client a chance to say she loved him one last time.

They didn't have a lovey-dovey relationship, so for her to come out and say those words to her usually lighthearted, non-sentimental brother was huge. His intuitive dream changed how she responded, and it made her act in a way that prevented future regret.

This is the mysterious aspect of intuition; it seems to be connected to so much more than ourselves. Intuition gives us a glimpse into the synchronicities we become a part of and our role in it all. Though we cannot always change what happens to us, intuition lends an opportunity to lessen the blows of the harshities of life.

Just as intuition gives us flashes of knowingness, it can also subtly guide our lives down the road of synchronicity. There have been countless moments where my intuition "pinged" at something that seemed to reoccur in my life, only for it to be brought up in a reading later. For example, in my televised reading with Marlee Matlin, I had a synchronistic hit before I even got there. As we turned the corner down her street, I saw a road sign that said SARAH ST., and my intuition indicated to me that that name would be significant in the reading. I was noticing it for a reason, and intuition was that reason. When I showed up to the reading, Marlee verified that "Sarah" not only applied to her family, but there was a "Sarah" in her sign language interpreter Jack's reading as well! This demonstrated the power of synchronicity to provide insight.

Similarly, I did a reading when I was just seventeen that made me look a little closer at coincidence. The reading was filmed in my hometown, with a young woman only a little older than me, named Navi. Navi's brother had passed away tragically years before, and her goal of the reading was to learn if her departed brother was aware of the things the family does to keep his memory alive.

From the moment I woke up that morning, I began noticing the strangest thing. I turned on the television, and a basketball game was going on. The camera zoomed in on one of the jerseys in a way that resembled a cameraman error. I changed the channel and didn't think much of it. Then, I went onto my phone and checked social media. As I browsed through, I noticed an advertisement for custom jerseys pop up on my screen. Funny, I thought, considering I'd just seen the weird jersey close-up on television.

I didn't think much more of it, and went about my day. When I got into the car to go to the reading, the radio turned on and I looked at the title of what was playing. "Jersey Girl" by Bruce Springsteen, was the first song to play when the car was turned on, and I was struck by how oddly my day was going.

To make matters even stranger, when I got to the set there was a single piece of litter at my feet. It was a sandwich wrapper from Jersey Mike's. At this point, I knew there definitely had to be something to all of these jersey references. I was just hoping it'd make sense to the client!

When I met with Navi, her brother was a clear communicator. One of the first things he acknowledged was the image of a blue and white jersey, hanging up on a wall. As I said this, she became incredibly emotional. Her brother had played basketball, and to honor him her family had framed his basketball jersey. Chills came over me when I realized that parts of my day leading up to the reading had been a message. It made me wonder about all of the other times a sign was sent that went unnoticed.

When our intuition isn't realized consciously, it can communicate to our subconscious through dreams. Countless great minds have credited dreams with giving insight into the waking world. At least one even resided in the White House! Abraham Lincoln had a dream that "strangely annoyed" him. He dreamt of a wooden coffin in the East Wing of the White House, with a Union soldier standing guard. In the dream, Lincoln asked the guard who was in the casket, and he responded, "The President. He has been killed by an assassin." Only three days after recounting this dream, Lincoln was assassinated and his body laid in the East Wing to await burial.

I have experienced intuition glimpses into the future through dreams. A few years ago, I had a dream that particularly struck me. Normally, my dreamtime is spent in a partially lucid state with little going on. This dream was different. In it, I was standing outside of my parents' home, looking into the garage window. As I looked closer, I realized the window was smashed and shards laid on the cement outside. Then, as I looked carefully, I observed as a man and a woman broke into the home through the back door and began stealing. The woman was having a good time and making a surprising amount of noise for a burglar.

I was jolted awake. Immediately, I knew this was no random dream. I called my dad within moments of waking and told him he needed to get more security for that part of the house. He took it seriously and said he'd look into getting precautionary measures installed in the coming weeks. He didn't act fast enough.

Less than three weeks after this dream, my parents' home was burglarized while they were out. This had never happened before. Upon inspecting the crime scene, the burglars had busted through the garage window and made their entry through the back door. Initially, it wasn't known how many people were involved, or who they were.

As I walked around the house, feeling both violated and equally impressed with myself, I realized something was missing. My hair products. A few weeks before, I'd been gifted high-end shampoo and conditioners from my friend Chaz Dean. As I looked around searching for my haircare, it struck me: what man would steal shampoo and conditioner?!

Ultimately, the people who broke into my parents' home were identified, and one of them jailed. Indeed, the girlfriend of the main assailant had joined in the burglary. Every aspect of my dream proved to be correct, and it made me never second-guess a dream again. When our intuition can't get our conscious attention, it'll find ways to plant seeds in the subconscious. Through nurturing and maintenance, intuition can grow.

Like any other skill, intuition can be improved through practice. While our ego and its narratives sometimes distract our consciousness, our intuition is always there. When we're quiet enough, we can hear it. There's something to be said about the importance of stillness in being a proper intuitive receiver. In a reading, I have to quiet my own thoughts and awareness of my body to do my job effectively. I always say that, in a reading, my body and mind are like a canvas, and the spirits paint the picture.

This concept is not a new one. The idea of purifying oneself of individual thoughts and feelings to be in alignment with a higher power is a universal concept. Everyone has different ways of reaching this state, and scribbling is mine. As bizarre as it sounds, the US government showed interest in this very concept in their study of remote viewing. In 1978, the Defense Intelligence Agency created Project Star Gate, a program dedicated to learning if intuiting details about faraway places was possible. The goal was to weaponize psychic abilities and create psychic spies.

It may sound far-fetched, but the program was only defunded in the nineties, when it was exposed to mainstream criticism. People involved in the program believe that it still exists today and was simply renamed and classified. Regardless, the US and Russian governments spent millions of tax dollars and decades of research to study this anomalous field. There are conflicting reports of the perceived effectiveness of remote viewing, but the evidence exists. There are plenty of declassified documents that can be downloaded and read from the CIA website that refer to transcripts of these insightful sessions.

The goal of the remote viewer was to intuit information about a destination thousands of miles away. The intuitive would be given only coordinates to focus on, and after the viewer cleared their mind, the coordinates would invoke strong mental images. You might be wondering how the government found individuals to test remote viewing, and the answer is as fascinating as the program itself. According to researcher Paul H. Smith, individuals were approached to be in the program if they had a military background coupled with a specific set of strengths. Particularly, individuals who were creative, musically inclined, good writers, and bilingual all seemed to be "better" at remote viewing, according to the government.

How they came to this conclusion is a mystery. I think it probably relates to the fact that intuitive thinking requires an integration of different ways of thinking. Those who are good at conceptualizing, visualizing, and retaining information all may make natural remote viewers. Smith also acknowledged that before a remote viewing session, many of the participants had certain rituals that they'd do to get into the intuitive mindset.

Scribbling was one of the primary "rituals" to get started, while others took more eccentric approaches. One man only listened to specific death metal when he was about to do a remote viewing session. So much for clearing your mind! A female participant always wore her "lucky" socks on the days she knew she'd be expected to remote view. As you can see, the processes these individuals used to tune in were just as unique as they were. There was no right or wrong way to do it, so long as it resulted in successful remote viewing.

One interesting issue the remote viewers dealt with was what was called overlay. Overlay would happen when the viewer jumped to a conclusion about the intuitive information they were receiving. If the target they were focusing on was white and palatial, they had to prevent themselves from assuming it was the White House. Very quickly, the viewers noticed that intuitive information could be misinterpreted if diluted with logical overlay. Viewers were encouraged to describe the target, not label it. The more they could avoid assumptions and stick to the information, the more successful the session went.

Also, the program revealed an incredibly high rate of psychic burnout. Participants had to resist the temptation of wanting to go "on a roll" when a particularly strong vision was verified as correct. It was essential to take breaks between sessions, and sometimes go days without trying at all. Strangely, beginners often had extremely validating strings of successful hits about the target. Meanwhile, the experienced viewer might stumble or need to do readings in intervals. Whether it's beginner's luck or something more, it's important to not get carried away with the rush of accuracy. The more mindful we can be every step of the way, the better off we'll be in the long run. Developing your spirituality isn't a sprint, it's a marathon. It'll follow you for the rest of your life if you're willing to take it by the hand. Like with all things, balance is essential. Much like how it's counterproductive to stress over meditating properly, it's equally important that you don't burn out on building intuitive structures.

The truths gleaned from Project Star Gate give us an interesting insight into our own spiritual work. While most of us don't have aspirations for psychic spying, there's value in what we can learn from their processes. When we can implement certain intuitive routines, we create a platform to build our intuition. If we can be mindful of the conclusions our brain is likely to jump to, then we can be more aware of intuition versus overlay.

Speaking of intuitive routines, let's talk about psychic tools. Tarot cards, crystal balls, and automatic writing are all attributed to psychics and mediums. At face value, these methods can seem a little dubious and evoke images of stereotypical fortune-tellers.

The reality is that these tools have a history that's been greatly misunderstood. At thirteen years old, I was gifted my first deck of tarot cards for my birthday. Initially, I, too, was hesitant around the idea of there being a "Death" card, and it all seemed very much like the beginning of a scary movie. The more I read about tarot, though, the more I began to understand the concept. The cards are just laminated pieces of paper with images on them, meant to evoke a certain feeling or idea that may be intuitive. The cards themselves aren't explicitly mystical, they are only as powerful as the person who wields them.

As I practiced with tarot cards more, I began to realize

that the images in the cards were symbolic. There were seventy-eight cards total, separated into minor and major arcana, meaning little and big secrets. When a person set their intention to a question or topic, they could pull a card and glean insight about it through what the cards brought to their attention.

It really didn't seem that otherworldly once I started familiarizing myself with the world of tarot. Originally popularized as a card game, tarot wasn't created with mystical intentions. Though some mystics used them for divination purposes for hundreds of years, the mainstream idea of tarot being a psychic tool is a relatively new one. Only around the turn of the century was the Rider-Waite tarot created, which illustrated the creation of the symbols we find in most modern tarot decks. It was a way of thinking of situations in a new way, and the randomness of the cards that were pulled meant that there was some element left open to fate. The combination of the card selected by chance, and the ideas that were evoked from the card's first impression, were both intuitive.

In becoming more aware of the tools that existed to instill and refine intuition, I broadened my horizons. I learned about scrying, the ancient origin of the crystal ball stereotype. Nostradamus, famed sixteenth-century French psychic, utilized scrying as a way of telling the future. To do this, he'd fill a bowl of water up and light some candles. Once night fell, he'd stare into the bowl of water and let his focus go. In a form of open-eyed meditation, he'd begin noticing certain visions and images play out on the still surface of the water. This was scrying. Historically, black mirrors, dark caves, and yes, crystal balls, have all been used as a means to zone out and tune in.

So, too, has the use of automatic writing, or the process of entering into a trance and writing unconsciously. The idea is that if this can be done properly, messages will be intercepted or delivered from the ether, and will be written on the page. This is a tool for insight popularized by the Spiritualism movement, and exemplified in the works of Brazilian medium Chico Xavier. Xavier is the most famous medium to come out of South America, and his process was fascinating. He'd write elaborate letters from the departed and hand them to the grieving person he was reading. He wrote down mind-blowing information, referring to intimate details of people's lives and last words. In one instance, two cynics came to debunk him and booked a reading with him. Giving him a fake name, the debunkers hoped he'd relay a bunch of nonsense or not be able to perform at all. They later reported to a local newspaper that upon scribbling, Xavier wrote both of their full names on a piece of paper and busted the cynics for being fraudulent themselves.

While I learned about psychic tools and those who used them, I found that altering one's senses through mystical practice was a common theme. Scryers stare into a dark, reflective object until images are evoked.

Tarot card readers do the same, by looking at a card with "new eyes," being mindful of only what seems to stand out or call out for attention.

This idea has been popularized in recent years through the creation of sensory deprivation tanks. In what is probably the most Californian invention next to kale chips, sensory deprivation tanks are used to quiet our senses, with the goal of reaching an altered state of consciousness. The tanks fit one's entire body, and they're filled with saltwater that matches the exact temperature of the person inside it. The tank is closed once the person is in it, making for a dark environment in which a person floats on a cloud of nothingness.

The goal of sensory deprivation tanks is to eliminate sensory input. Static noise is sometimes played through speakers, to eliminate other auditory input. Being in this state for twenty to thirty minutes is supposed to have a therapeutic effect that gives the body a bit of a re-boot. Many individuals, however, have reported having strong visions and psychic experiences while floating. This concept is nothing new. Just like the monks who would venture into dark caves for days to receive messages from the Gods, sensory deprivation is an age-old concept that has always intuitively resonated. Why else would people do it?

In my journey through discovering these modalities of mystical experiences, I came upon an interesting concept called the Ganzfeld Effect. Popularized more than eighty years ago, the Ganzfeld Effect was a sensory deprivation practice to try to test telepathy, with surprisingly anomalous results. The idea was simple: cover the eyes of the participant with a semitransparent surface where light could shine through. Then, turn on a light behind the participant so that their vision can only see a faint glow and nothing else.

Then, the participant is to wear headphones with white noise being played, to drown out any auditory stimuli. After about twenty minutes, most individuals reported noticing some sensory information that came from somewhere else. Being the enthusiastic teenager I was, when I learned about the Ganzfeld Effect, I had to try it for myself. In fact, I did it regularly with a friend.

The process was an easy one. We'd cut in half a ping-pong ball and tape the halves to our eyes. We'd shine a red light from a lamp behind us and put in headphones with static noise. One person would keep watch and take notes, and the other would see what could be intuited. With ping pong balls taped to my eyes, I looked like the world's most mature horse fly. My experiments with the Ganzfeld Effect never led to any telepathic moments, but they did give me an insight into the goal of sensory deprivation, and how it ties into meditation.

No matter what the goal, be it psychic insight or peace of mind, the process is the same. The aim is to be a clear canvas for insight to be imprinted upon. Those impressions might be peaceful, or they might prove to be insightful. Sometimes even both.

With all of the tools at your disposal to initiate

psychic experiences, you mustn't forget that you're the most powerful vessel in your toolkit. All of the tools you have access to only work when you're present to work with them. As time has gone on, I've relied less on external tools for insight and have learned to go inward. There are external tools that are represented through what we've covered, but the world of inner tools at your disposal is boundless. When you can rely less on an external tool as a crutch, you'll be empowered in your intuition. By going inward, you can access that which exists just under the surface.

This is only possible if we can create an internal blank slate. The same mechanisms apply to all of us, and the more we can reduce external stimuli, the more we can notice the subtleties of our inner worlds. Mindfulness is a concept that has existed since the dawn of man, and there's a reason it's such a powerful tool for happiness. I define mindfulness as being able to get the most meaning out of the present moment. When we can quiet our thoughts about the past and our fears for the future, we're present.

Mindfulness is easier said than done. When was the last time you ate breakfast, spoon in hand, and really savored every bite you put in your mouth? So often in modern society, mindful opportunities are replaced with the blue light of our smartphones. Mindfulness is fundamentally experiential, as in, "Stop and smell the roses."

There are two meditative practices that help me be

more mindful. The first practice involves a little visualization, but it's a great way to shift your perspective from being defined by your thoughts, to observing them. To start, close your eyes and familiarize yourself with the darkness of your closed eyes. Take note of how your arms and legs feel, and notice if there's any tension in any particular part of your body. Make an effort to notice as much sensory input as possible. Smells, textures, physical tension, and posture are all things you can be aware of that will set your focus on yourself, which is the ultimate goal of this meditation. Go down a mental checklist and see what stimuli you most notice while your eyes are shut.

After a few moments of actively noticing stimuli and being more aware of your body, you might be a bit bored. At this point, it's time to visualize. In the darkness of your closed eyes, begin imagining that you're beside a running stream. Envision the rocks, the water, and the greenery that embody your mental picture. Quietly watch as the water trickles down the stream, while still letting thoughts pop in and pass through your mind.

Then, after you've created this mental landscape, it's time to start the real work. At this point, begin taking notice of any thoughts that come into your mind as you're watching the stream flow. If there's a thought that seems to be recurring, notice it.

Our ultimate goal is to take a recurring thought and turn it into a single image in our mind's eye. By simplifying a string of events or potentialities into a single image, we'll ultimately be able to have more control over it.

In our example, let's assume your recurring thought is about an unexpected bill you received in the mail earlier that you'll eventually have to pay. Take that memory and let your brain run through it a few times. Don't apply resistance, just let it come as you watch your stream. As your brain plays through receiving the mail, then opening it, then all of the thoughts about the anxiety it caused, try to slow down. Minimize that memory to a single image, if you can. Instead of thinking about everything that led up to receiving the bill and how you felt afterwards, try to focus on one distinct feature about the thought that's easy to focus on.

Maybe in our example, that one image that represents the bill most clearly in our head is the envelope it came in. When you can successfully turn that thought into a single mental image, this is where the magic begins. From there, imagine that this token that represents your thought is now floating down the stream you've been watching in your mind's eye. Watch as that envelope (that represents the bill) begins flowing downstream, going further and further, until it's no longer in your field of view.

Turn any complex thought that you have, particularly one that recurs, into a simple image. You can still think the thought freely, but turn it into a visual representation that's just one image. Watch as whichever image you select goes from upstream to downstream, and you'll notice a funny thing begins to happen.

When you've turned your thought into an image and watched that image from the perspective of an observer, a narrative shift happens. You go from actively experiencing the memory or trauma, to watching it float down a stream and away from you. The stream represents your consciousness, and as you simplify complex thoughts into a digestible token, you'll notice mindfulness becomes a lot easier. Visualization is powerful, and doing this meditation can help us be the observer and minimize the emotional impact of painful memories. If your recurring thought is of what you have to do later, turn that thought into a picture. Maybe you have homework to tend to—turn that thought into a single sheet of paper, floating down your stream.

If the subject of your thoughts falls onto a person, let yourself think of them. You can turn them into a single picture, too. Imagine a print-out of their face, or an article of their clothing, floating down your mental stream until it's no longer visible. As you can see, the point of this meditation is to take complicated thoughts and transform them into simple symbols that we can mentally watch wash away.

The second meditation I'll recommend is one I do every single day. It's called a cord-cutting exercise, and it works off of a similar premise as the stream meditation. The specific purpose of cord-cutting meditations is to quiet our thoughts entirely. While the stream meditation makes us more mindful of our thoughts and our role as the observer, the goal of cord-cutting is to remove a thought altogether.

This can be immensely helpful for those who deal with intrusive thoughts or have nagging feelings they can't find relief from. It only requires a little visualization! Just like the first meditation, close your eyes and become oriented with your physical body. After a few moments of familiarizing yourself with your headspace, let your thoughts flow with no real expectation. See what pops in, gets mulled over briefly, and then pops out. You might notice some thoughts seem to reoccur.

Once you've got a thought you want to get rid of, try to turn it into a single image. Imagine that a red cord connects to your chest and extends thirty feet into the darkness of your vision. At the end of that red cord, visualize a single image that connects at the end of it, floating in the void. Once you've turned your thought into a picture that's now floating attached to the red cord, it's time to cut it.

Visualize the biggest pair of golden shears you've ever seen, and imagine them cutting the cord that connects you to whatever image you've got in mind. Watch as that image floats away from you the moment the cord is cut, falling into the darkness, never to return again. Imagine what sounds the shears make when they cut the cord, the more detail the better. As you let the image fall into the darkness, you'll notice that another thought eventually replaces it. That's the point. Turn the following thought into an image, and repeat until there're noticeable gaps between the thoughts that come into your mind. It's a surreal feeling once it starts working, and it's immensely helpful in establishing both mindfulness and control over your thoughts. I used to scoff at the idea of visualization being a powerful tool for inner work, but even I was surprised by how much these practices transformed my own life and perspective. By taking a memory and turning it into a symbol that we witness outside of ourselves, we can more easily manage the thought at hand.

All of these practices are helpful to do throughout your day, and as you become more adept at them, you'll notice that practicing them becomes almost instinctual. The point is to ultimately quiet the mind through asserting control over it. When we can do this successfully, even for a few seconds, we usually don't realize it until we're already out of it. This is the aim of most meditation, to obtain a state of mind that transcends our thoughts about the past and future.

Ultimately, there's great value in slowing life down. When we're able to reduce the business of our day-to-day life, we become receptive to things we weren't before, like our intuition. Many spiritual beliefs emphasize the importance of stillness and its relationship with balance. Life is in motion, and our lives are full of action. Meditation counters this with a conscious slowing of the roll, enabling us to wrangle our restless consciousness.

Sometimes, we slip into mindful states without even

realizing it. I was guilty of finding my mindful moments in high school through daydreaming in class, letting my mind flow wherever it wanted until the stream of consciousness slowed. That may be great for inner peace, but not sublime in scoring high on tests.

Taoists honor the importance of something called "the flow state." We enter into this state of mind when we're doing an activity that makes us lose our sense of time. Dancers, pianists, and professional swimmers can all relate to getting into the flow state, because their focus has to be almost entirely on what they're doing. Similarly, we enter into this when we're reading a captivating book or listening to our favorite music. Humans crave the flow state, and implementing more activities that get you there is essential to mindful living. The more you can familiarize yourself with this headspace through activities, the more control you'll have in applying this mindset to other things, like intuitive development.

Take note of how you feel when doing something that gets you in your flow. Try to consciously notice the difference between doing things that make time feel nonexistent and doing things that make time drag on. Joy can be found in immersing yourself in timeless mindful activities. So, too, can learning what brings you peace.

While we're discussing mindful activities, let's talk about meditation. I find that most people put way too much expectation on meditating, which defeats the purpose. It isn't something you should have to find the time to do, it should be a lifestyle habit that you maintain daily. You don't need to meditate for an hour a day. In fact, you don't even need to meditate for ten minutes a day. Finding sacred alone time throughout your routine for only a few minutes is more realistic, and easier to implement. Take three minutes in the morning to focus on your breathing, focus on your center, and try to be the mindful observer of your thoughts. You can do this while you brush your teeth, but make sure you don't fall asleep.

Spacing out these little opportunities for meditation is an integral part of making meditation a lifestyle. I meditate nearly every morning as I'm driving to go get coffee. I put my time in the passenger seat to good use, and don't waste time getting riled up about my responsibilities for the day. I know what has to be done, but I also know the importance of starting the day on the right foot. Mindful meditation time allows us to train ourselves to go inward in a world that can be outwardly demanding.

Along with mindfulness, practice is fundamental to developing intuition. So many times, people will get intuitive hunches only to blow them off. By not putting our intuition into practice, we waste what it has to offer us. As you make mindfulness more of a priority throughout your life, notice the times when your inner voice tries to speak up. It might be trying to tell you something. As you create a blank canvas for yourself, you'll be able to see what picture is being painted for you to look at.

As a child, I practiced my intuition obsessively. I'd try to quiet my mind and then read random people on the street, and often naively delivered messages. I don't recommend doing the same. By making the focus of your intuition yourself, you can strengthen your inner relationship and create a framework to channel it. When you get ready in the morning, ask yourself what colors you feel called to wear. Go with your gut.

As you get ready to leave for work, ask yourself what time feels right to leave. Follow that time through and take note of any synchronicities along the way. As you determine which route you'll go to work, check in with yourself and see what feels most efficient.

There's a million ways to practice your intuition, but it can only be done when you've achieved some familiarity with mindfulness. As you become more receptive to intuitive hunches, it becomes important to trust in what your practice teaches you. A message is useless if you don't trust it enough to follow through with what it says.

Intuition is a powerful tool, but we have limitations in the extent that we can harness it. As you notice your intuition increasing through practice, it's easy to become overconfident in one's abilities. This internal compass doesn't make us all-knowing. It can act as a guide for insight, but all individuals ultimately have blind spots. You can learn as much from your blind spots as you can from your accurate validations, and it's important to not be afraid of dealing with these. The ego may want to deem an intuitive blind spot as being "wrong," but you mustn't be critical in your practice. Nobody is 100 percent, and there are spiritual laws in place that prevent us from knowing what we aren't supposed to know.

I witnessed a powerful demonstration of this in a reading I did recently. A young man reached out to me for a reading for himself and his fiancée. He and she were newly engaged, and they wanted to see if I could provide any insight into the trajectory of their future. Being a medium, my role is to communicate with spirits, but sometimes insight can be gleaned from the path someone is presently on. Through intuitive hunches about the present, one can infer aspects of the future.

This was the goal of the reading. As I met with the soon-to-be husband and wife, I saw a full gamut of information about their past and present plans. I intuited details about their departed loved ones and brought through information about how they met and some of the difficulties they had dealt with. I accurately described their plans for the future and the exact number of kids they wanted to have. I didn't necessarily see this happening, but I saw that the present moment seemed to be leading them that direction based on their intentions.

All in all, it was a great reading by my standards. They left the experience having reconnected with loved ones and feeling further validation of their bond together. The reading highlighted both their strengths and what could be improved upon, and left them with a better understanding of how to move forward. This is the aim for every reading.

Right before we parted ways, the man remembered a question he'd forgotten during the reading. He asked about an upcoming trip his fiancée and he were taking to Indonesia and China. The plan was to spend a week in each place, starting with Jakarta and then traveling up to Beijing. When he spoke, a strange feeling came over me, like I was being distracted. I determined that his vacation would be cut short in Indonesia, and though I couldn't determine why, I told him to be mindful of this and to not expect a vacation in China.

He seemed a little put off by the statement, and I felt awkward. I acknowledged that it might not be for any concerning reason and might just be a surprise change of plans that neither of us were anticipating.

In some ways, I was correct. I was blindsided with the news that their vacation was cut short in Jakarta. Four days into their trip, they got into a car accident and his fiancée was killed suddenly. I had seen her only days prior, and yet the information about her impending death was kept from me.

It was one of many similarly painful experiences I'd go through, akin to the Alan Thicke reading. I'm reminded regularly that as the messenger for information, I only have access to so much. Through my work I've come to understand that certain things cannot be prevented, and certain processes cannot be interrupted. There are universal laws at play that prevent us from being all-knowing, despite what intuition can reveal.

Sometimes, we aren't meant to know something at a particular moment in time, and then that changes. Very often, if I'm unable to get a psychic impression about one aspect of a person's life, I'll ask to speak with them in six months' time. After a period of time has passed, I'll sometimes be able to glean new information about a subject that once evaded me.

I've noticed this happens particularly on readings for pregnant women. The question usually comes up as to whether the baby is going to be a boy or a girl, and I have a pretty solid accuracy rate from past predictions. But often, I can only get that answer after a period of time. Sometimes I can predict babies years in advance, as seen in countless readings on my show. Other times, a woman has to get to a particular stage in her pregnancy for me to "get" information about the baby. Though time isn't a limitation to those on the other side, there do seem to be some time-based limitations for us in this realm. Information can be communicated instantaneously from our intuition, but there're also times where our attempts are rendered useless and that's that. Either way, you have to trust the process and not let your ego become frustrated. A personal mantra of mine is: "I'll know what I know when I know it."

I have to trust immensely in every reading I do. I can't be worried about how I could look if I'm wrong, or even what the client is expecting to get out of the experience.

I must be focused on the present moment in its entirety. As you develop your intuition and you begin noticing the times when you've correctly interpreted it, incredible shifts begin to occur. Doors seem to open. Intuitive hunches are catalysts for great change. When we can go from a faith-based mindset around spirituality to a trust-based one, a transformation of perspective occurs. When we see the power our intuition possesses and the implications that has on our place in the universe, doubt is erased altogether. Intuition affirms to us our role in the world and aids us in reaching new heights.

One of the beautiful aspects of embracing our inner-tuition is that it can help us get the most out of life. It can prevent us from living with regret that we would otherwise have. When we can acknowledge it, it reminds us that we are extensions of the divine. Material problems and temporary issues become easier to deal with when the curtain is pulled back, ever so briefly, to show us the true nature of reality. If your intuition does not inspire you to know yourself and make great change, then it is not intuition. All practices utilized to refine it should send us on a productive path of self-knowingness and confidence.

No matter where you are in your inward journey, we all have strengths to refine. Everybody has something to offer in the qualities we bring to the table. When you can confidently step in the direction of self-discovery, you rely less on the external for answers. Guidance, trust, and divine purpose are all accessible through yourself.

4

Align with Your Authenticity

Authenticity Is Alignment

"If you don't know who you truly are, you'll never know what you really want."

—*Roy T. Bennett*

What does being authentic mean to you? Honest, sincere, and real might be adjectives that come to mind. But being true to who we are—embracing our passions, interests, fears, and quirks, regardless of whether they're commonly accepted—is real authenticity. This is what we should all be striving for: not just because authenticity is a likeable personality trait but because it's a major factor in finding true fulfillment in our lives.

Of course, this is easier said than done in a world that pushes its standards upon us and forces us into systems of social rank and self-comparison. Nowhere is this better exemplified than on social media, with its universe of filters, social pressure, and fabricated reality.

Many people are afraid to be authentically themselves, both online and in the real world, out of fear of not being good enough. On the other end of the spectrum, inauthenticity can lead to rewards for those acting disingenuously, which only warps and inflates their ego more.

We all harness varying degrees of authenticity about different aspects of ourselves. The more we know ourselves, the more we can see what's true to ourselves. If we're not aware of what's motivating our actions, we run the risk of doing things that go against our authentic wishes. The more you can know what you want, the more you can get what you want.

Living authentically is also about living mindfully. When we are aware of the present moment and the narratives at play within it, we have the truest understanding of what's informing our reality. We can be honest with others as well as ourselves. Striving for the truth of all things is the nature of intuitive living.

In many of my communications with the departed, they have underscored the dangers of self-comparison, of living our lives for other people, and of harmful self-talk that prevents us from expressing what's true to ourselves. Those who live in alignment with their souls make waves, from Martin Luther King, Jr., to Harvey Milk, to Maya Angelou. Some of the most inspiring minds on Earth sparked revolutions simply by being themselves—and fighting for a greater good that outlived their physical bodies and united them all. Many of their plights were motivated by God, intuition, or some greater calling that they felt the need to answer.

Living authentically doesn't have to get us into history books to be fulfilling; in fact, most people who live authentically tend not to waste time with external validation. One example of this took place during a reading I did with a woman who was trying to contact her departed grandmother. Given the number of grandmothers I've brought through over the course of a thousand readings, I've lost count of how many knit goods and homemade recipes they've mentioned. This grandma was different, which I noticed right away from the object her granddaughter handed me to contact her: a mangled brown leather glove. As her grandmother came through, I saw black smoke and machinery accompanied by the loud revving of an engine. As I communicated this, my client explained that the woman she called Grandma had been a mechanic her entire life, pursuing that career despite pressure from both her parents and society to do something else. She remained unmarried and decided (also against her family's wishes) to adopt my client's mother—an African American baby—in the 1950s . . . in rural Alabama. As a white woman living amid the hatred and segregation of the south, she made an incredibly risky and equally meaningful choice to follow her truth for the greater good.

When the grandmother came through, she communicated that following her heart wasn't easy, but that was what made it most worthwhile. Nothing of value was gained easily; every challenge was an opportunity. She was only able to recognize all of this by staying true to who she was. However, she also acknowledged that she learned from those experiences, and understood that for every person that shunned her for being who she was, it made room for someone to come into her life and love her more than the previous person ever could have. She realized that living authentically thinned out those who didn't truly resonate with her and attracted those who did. In this way, being herself had an alchemical quality in her life. It transformed her surroundings when she went out on a limb and did something she knew was right. My client's grandmother was a true example of how living genuinely makes ripples for generations to come.

When we live authentically, we do not hide from our emotions. We do not project, as there is no need. We are not defensive; we are simply true to who we are. This chapter will explore the theme of authenticity and what I've learned about it throughout my work as a medium.

No one is born insecure. From the moment our consciousness realizes the world, we begin to be shaped by it. We respond to positive reinforcement and negative reinforcement. As we get older, we come to certain conclusions about morality and the definition of good and bad. Our understandings of these concepts are molded by our guardians and the societal norms of the times we exist in. When we deem something negative, every interaction with that thing invokes negative emotions. We're deterred from that which we deem bad, and therefore unpleasant.

This becomes a problem when we feel bad about ourselves. Certain insecurities can develop through the conditioning we acquire. Sometimes, our life experiences distort how we view ourselves and others, and that can be a problematic informant to our actions. When we're supported as children, we feel capable of supporting ourselves. If we're shut down as children, we feel minimized and unheard. All childhoods have a combination of helpful and harmful experiences. The resilience we show despite whatever hardship we face is the sum of it all. It can be easy to recognize our beliefs about things in the external world. Our likes and dislikes and the things we find stimulating or interesting are all pretty straightforward to identify for most of us. Yet it's our inner self-beliefs that can be hardest to pin down. Many of the beliefs we hold about ourselves are ingrained in us, from years of conditioning. We may have told ourselves a certain narrative so many times that we don't even realize that was the case. Our beliefs become embedded in the filter we see the world through.

With every societal role we take on, we lean on certain beliefs about ourselves for support. When we're needed in our occupation, a certain degree of self-belief is required to get the job done. When we're needed interpersonally, we bring certain strengths and weaknesses to the table and believe in our extent to effectively communicate. Yet, certain external factors shape and mold our self-belief, and we must always be cognizant of that which makes us feel insecure.

One of the greatest hindrances to authentic living can be found in unfounded fear. Fear of how others may react and fear of our own ability to handle problems heavily shapes our decision-making, even subconsciously. I argue that we should make use of our fear by bringing it out of the shadows and into the light. In many spiritual circles, fear is viewed as the enemy, and love is believed to be all there truly is.

I'm not of that belief. I believe fear is an incredible tool for spiritual growth and should be embraced, not ignored. Fear of getting hit by a car is why you look both ways when you cross the street. If it weren't for fear, we wouldn't know what to avoid, and what, in turn, might harm us.

The issue becomes when we live in perpetual states of fear. When certain triggers have so much power over us that they can change the course of our entire day, that time adds up. Coping with fear and negative self-talk eats away at the experiencer and steals the saturation from the color of life. Oftentimes, much of our fear is rooted in our conditioning. Trauma, pressure, and self-imposed expectations of how things should be can all contribute to what makes us afraid. Fear can also obviously be caused by malfunctions in the brain, as seen in OCD and clinical depression. In cases like this, it's important to consider what can be done to achieve greater balance through psychology and psychiatry. No matter how much you work on yourself, if your mental health struggles require medical help, you should heed that call. There's no shame in taking medicine for an illness or working things out with a professional.

When we can determine the root of what makes us afraid, we're empowered. Even if we aren't eliminating our fear, just knowing what's causing it and what it's rooted in can help us feel more in control. This is only possible when we're self-aware, and many people have problems they never know the source of. In knowing yourself, you're one step closer to a solution. Though many are afraid to delve into the ins and outs of who we are, this should be a goal you seek to fulfill every single day. Carl Jung emphasized the importance of integrating our self and our persona so that we aren't defined by what's repressed in the unconscious mind. All too often, people fall victim to their own cycles and behavior, and self-awareness will get you further than any work you could possibly do externally.

Much of what we fear revolves around shame. I've seen time and time again the power of shame in the life of individuals, both in readings and on the other side. Holding on to shame, particularly for long periods, can put a person into mental atrophy and dim their spark for life. Much of shame is caused by previous experiences that have made one feel ashamed. To avoid future shame, people repress the decidedly negative quality and live with a thorn in their side.

One of my favorite quotes about dealing with naysayers comes from Theodore Roosevelt. He said:

> It is not the critic who counts; not the man who points out how the strong man stumbles, or where the doer of deeds could have done them better. The credit belongs to the man who is actually in the arena, whose face is marred by dust and sweat and blood; who strives valiantly; who errs, who comes short again and again, because there is no effort without error and shortcoming; but who does actually strive to do the deeds; who knows great enthusiasms, the great devotions; who spends himself in a worthy cause; who at the best knows in the end the triumph of high achievement, and who at the worst, if he fails, at least fails while daring greatly, so that his place shall never be with those cold and timid souls who neither know victory nor defeat.

The essence of this quote is that authenticity requires courage, and those who spend all of their time criticizing take the lazy route through life, never truly living, while belittling those who do. It is not your job to please the world, your job is to change the world you live in in whatever way, big or small, that you can. The only way that we can recognize what we're destined to do is if we're willing to risk being authentic. Every mover and changer the world has ever seen has faced pushback.

Sometimes, that pushback acted as inspiration for ingenuity through competition. How we frame criticism is an important factor in how we ultimately view it as a whole. We can let it destroy our self-esteem, or we can be self-assured in who we know we truly are, and consider it with grace, but never be defined by it. You should aim to take criticism into consideration, but know yourself, your strength, and your truth to the extent that nothing can truly shake your core. When we step into our purpose and put fear aside, we can change ourselves and better the collective as a result.

The path to self-assuredness isn't an easy one. We live in a traumatic world. It can be hard to apply confidence in the face of unpredictability, but intuition can help us through uncertainty. As we get in touch with our inner worlds, we begin to notice them calling out to us, begging to be self-realized and turned into something productive. The more you explore your consciousness, the more you'll be compelled to do. The more that we listen to our inner voice, the more we realize what passions exist within us, having gone undeveloped. We see the untapped potential and tap into it with confidence. We feel called to create, inspired to make change through our lens of existence. The more we know ourselves, the more we have to work with in executing our purpose.

You might be wondering by this point if we all have a single life purpose. I don't believe so. I've found through readings that our lives serve many purposes in many different respects. We wear many different hats and are a different person to everyone who knows us. I believe that our goal shouldn't be to stick to one life purpose, but to instead live purposefully in every moment. If you can live sentimentally and with mindfulness and diligence, life will take on extraordinary levels of meaning never previously accessed. Furthermore, when we feel more purposeful, we're empowered to take actions that lead to more purpose. The key is to find a way to shake off energetic atrophy and initiate change for yourself. It starts with you. Rather than always being a subject of other people's purpose, be the extension of your own.

Seizing the chances that are unique only to your circumstances instills a sense of purpose. The universe works through our specific hardships and opportunities. Having the mental wherewithal to respond, not react, to resistance is empowering. When we can view the world as a stage play that's performing to teach us something, our perspective shifts for the better.

Being a medium who happens to be gay, I'm often asked which was more difficult to honor in my life growing up. I've given varying answers, because the answer changes. Both were two drastically different things to come to terms with and have to be real about, to myself and to others. Though I grew up in a conservative town and went to a small school, other kids had heard of and seen gay people. I may have been the only one who was out at the time, but people had watched *Will & Grace*—they'd seen the homosexuals.

Coming out of the medium closet was a different story. People hadn't met mediums, and the closest depictions in film that they could relate to was *The Sixth Sense*. In many ways, it would have been easier to keep being a medium a secret. I could have quietly continued my life down the path I was headed, to become a hospice nurse.

The more I did readings in my teen years, the more I couldn't ignore my own intuition. Just as I could intuit messages for others, I knew when I was doing it that it simply felt right. When I was doing readings, time flew by, and I lived meaningfully. The same intuition that relayed messages from the other side guided me down the path I would find most fulfilling. Only by listening, and taking innumerable risks, was I able to step into my purpose.

When I first told my dad about my ability, it took some getting used to. Whenever I tell the story about my dad finding out about me being a medium, I highlight that he was ultimately receptive once he understood it. Initially though, my dad didn't want me to do readings outright. He ran a small business in our town, and there was legitimate concern that my readings would be detrimental to his livelihood.

So, I packed up my tarot cards and newly bought incense and threw it all haphazardly into the closet. I remember crying and feeling so conflicted, because of my knowingness that my purpose was to do readings, and yet my external circumstances weren't letting me fulfill that purpose. At that moment, I had no other option than to have faith. Circumstances prevented me from living my truth, but I couldn't ignore the truth itself. Even at the time, I knew that despite the rejection I was facing, I would go on to heed the call.

And I did. It took time, but eventually as the weeks passed, I fished the tarot cards and incense out of the closet and began spending more time quietly practicing. I was met with resistance from people at school and those in my community. From every angle I was being pressured to find a more realistic career and to not limit my occupational horizons. After a school counselor singled me out and told me a fellow student called me creepy, he asked me, "Well, are you?"

That horrible question embodied my high school experience. Adults were just as juvenile as the students. As a child I'd always gone to adults for guidance, yet by high school I had reached a point where adults were no longer a safe place to fall. Always feeling like the outsider and never feeling understood felt like my cross to bear. My experiences with bullying from adults and students prepared me for the world and the media, and it was one of many examples of a need for strong self-esteem.

The very skillset I was bullied relentlessly for is the one I'll be remembered for. No matter what backlash I faced, I listened to the call that said it was all worth something greater. Even during the times when I saw no potential way out of the horrible feelings these situations instilled, I knew viscerally that it would all lead to brighter days.

I never saw the light at the end of the tunnel, but my intuition said it was there. Because I listened to it, and was willing to take the risks it encompasses, I was able to step into the most purposeful life possible. As a teenager, I knew my purpose was to help grieving people and their loved ones. At sixteen, the most practical application of this seemed to be hospice nursing. Though I didn't see the career that was ahead for me, I had an understanding of a goal that has never changed. My purpose was realized, and the universe ultimately sent the perfect platform for others to realize it, too. This isn't unique to me—when we display the courage that authenticity requires, a whole chain of events gets set into place. If we can continually apply courage and strength, then we build upon this chain and consciously climb up the ladder of success.

I realized through my work that the departed put a huge emphasis on living authentically. No matter what type of personality someone possessed at the time of death, they all came through with some developed understanding of their true nature. In life, people are able to distract themselves from that which they don't want to look at. When you die, there're no distractions to lean on. The departed must look at things objectively and see reality for what it is, integrated with multiple perspectives.

When I was in the midst of making my own career choices at seventeen, I had a reading with a client that delivered a message not only to her, but to me as well. The client was a middle-aged woman named Deborah, whose mother had died six months prior to the reading. Deborah's mother had lived to be a centenarian, passing away at 104 years old. She spent the last thirty years of her life nearly wheelchair bound, and wasn't happy for a long time. In fact, Deborah said, her mother had been depressed all throughout Deborah's childhood.

As the elder came through to me, she communicated a full life, in a physical sense. I could tell that her name was Marcia and that she was a homebody. I could feel the length of her days; her energy felt like an encyclopedia of information and memories. Though I was impressed with the extent of her resilience to live over a century, I couldn't help but feel something was missing. The more I lingered in her essence, the more uncomfortable I became. She showed me multiple situations in which her younger self ignored meaningful opportunities, only for them to never return.

In one instance, she highlighted a situation involving her first love, a young man who truly loved her. They'd met when she was in high school, and it was love at first sight. Despite her adoration for him, she was so caught up in her family's approval, as was common in those days, that she passed up the opportunity of a lifetime. She rejected her love interest without even running it by her parents, assuming that her father wouldn't like him.

Their love was never to be. The man went on to meet another woman, fall madly in love, and enter a marriage that would last for over fifty years. She spent her life always trying to fill the space his absence created. She lived with regret over her decision and never truly felt romantic love again. Her parents went on to pass away only six months after she rejected her love interest, rendering their approval or lack thereof completely null in the grand scheme.

Her soul recognized a self-sabotaging trait in herself, as there were other opportunities throughout her life that she rationalized away and didn't take. In her life review, she was taken back to a moment in her thirties when a dog was crossing through a busy street, and she continued to drive on and let someone else worry about it. She realized the chance that was put in front of her to do good, and saw that she had rejected that opportunity.

Through her life review process, she saw that much of her life was spent finding excuses. And oftentimes, they were good excuses that seemed to fulfill a need for a rational approach. Not pursuing her love interest seemed practical because she wrongly assumed that she needed her parent's approval to love someone. Not stopping for the dog in the street seemed logical because it was a busy road, and surely there'd be other people to do it.

But none of that mattered. She spent her life rationalizing her shortcomings so much so that she never even recognized them as shortcomings. She blamed the world for her problems and became as ill mentally as she was physically in her older age. Not only did she miss out on seeing the heart of every situation, she relinquished accountability by calling it fate.

On the other side, Marcia seemed to realize much of what her ego prevented her from seeing. She saw how she got in her own way, and the extent that she was a detriment to her own happiness. She was in the process of finding acceptance about her life at the time that we spoke, but it was still very much happening. She still acknowledged some regret about how she lived her life. She was granted 104 years on this planet, and yet she recognized that many who had lived shorter lives lived more meaningfully than she ever did. She saw in her life review process that life was about quality, not quantity. She felt like she had wasted enriching opportunities. She ultimately came to understand the basis of all that informed her life, but her parting words to me left me uneasy.

"No matter how okay I become with how things went, I'll always remember that I could have done more."

Her words act as a reminder to me when I'm faced with situations where my help could be of use. Instances in which we're able to lend a helping hand are always remembered when we die. When the opportunity to extend compassion comes our way, no kind deed is meaningless. Our lives provide opportunities for us to extend compassion unique to what our situations allow, and we must strive to take every chance we can to look out for one another. Our life review doesn't emphasize the times you spent doing mindless work or distracting yourself, it reflects most the moments where fulfillment could have been increased. Just as we're faced with what we didn't do and could've done, we enjoy seeing the fruits of our compassionate labor. We see how every act of kindness, particularly selflessness, made the collective a better whole. We realize ourselves as part of the bigger picture, a mere extension of a greater unit. Souls on the other side eventually see the true nature of our existence and its entangled, interwoven nature that unites us.

Purposeful living involves approaching our lives with childlike enthusiasm and curiosity. Only then, when we are unafraid to ask questions and pursue answers, are we able to know what we really want out of our time. People's expectations of us can put us into boxes, and it's essential that we be willing to step out of others' limitations and think outside the box. Our interests are indications of our calling. What you feel pulled to do is an indicator of what you're here to do. Only when our interests are encouraged and supported can they flourish, and often that relies on a guardian to lift us up. Parents often inadvertently hurt their children, even if their intentions are good. Sometimes, children don't feel understood by those they look to for approval, and this can be damaging. We must strive to validate those who are called to do great things, not discourage them. Just because there may be an easier way doesn't mean the path of least resistance will lead to happiness.

I think a huge part of living authentically is being able to balance inner vision with the outer work that must be done. Often people get too caught up in how things should be, versus the reality of how they are. Perfectionists often want a do-over if things start off on the wrong foot. We have certain ideas of happiness and the way our lives should go for us to reach happiness.

However, the universe doesn't abide by our expectations. Wrenches get thrown. Rugs get pulled from underneath us. Our journey to self-discovery isn't seamless, and it'd be pointless if it was. Lessons come from navigating obstacles. Stepping out of our comfort zone is necessary to achieve anything worthwhile that we don't already have. Being able to go with the flow and apply resilience will get you further than thinking you have it all figured it out. When we let things be what they are, and only try to change what can be changed, we conserve our energy. Going with the flow through what we cannot change and taking life one day at a time serve us better than imposing stress on ourselves to fix the unfixable.

There's that "flow" word again. A huge part of finding purpose is being able to identify what gets us in our flow state. There's a spiritual quality to doing that which we feel called to do. We are the universe experiencing itself. When we engage in activities that get us into our flow, we become transcendent. The feeling of losing yourself in your favorite activity can be therapeutic. Dancers describe a feeling of losing track of time when in the middle of a riveting performance. So, too, do artists who immerse themselves in their craft. You enter into flow states when you daydream to your favorite song, or do anything that makes you feel entirely present. We're reminded of the timeless nature of reality, and that all that truly exists is the present. The hobbies, roles, and actions that inspire your flow are an essential part of your well-being.

The idea of living a purposeful life and a successful life are of the same vein. Both emphasize thriving where you're planted and achieving a sense of fulfillment. I define success as the realization and execution of our purposes. It's more than material excess or external validation; success is being able to die knowing you lived a life worth having.

In the following pages, I'll highlight two stories that drastically exemplify success, purpose, and the pursuit of happiness. The first involves one of the most affluent clients I've ever read, and the second a family in my hometown.

A few years ago, I visited Europe for the first time. A mysterious client who belonged to a socialite family reached out to my management for an in-person reading. I was asked for two hours of my time, and my mother and I were flown to the UK to meet someone I knew nothing about. As you can probably imagine, this was all very surreal.

We flew first class and arrived at the airport to a

private car; our trip was off to an opulent start. It embodied the kind of hollow materialism that would go on to define the experience. When it came time to meet my client, it was no small feat. After we pulled past the mansion gates, men with machine guns emerged from the complex. They walked around the vehicle and scanned underneath it. I later found out they were checking to make sure there were no bombs, or people, hitching a ride under the vehicle.

My client was at constant risk for kidnapping. Their family been bombed in the past, and this was a credible threat for them. Our passports were taken and scanned, and photographs of me and my mother were taken to be documented. We signed nondisclosure agreements with the understanding to never divulge their names.

Before I even met my client, it was made evident the bubble they lived in. To live an existence considered by most to be the dream was actually a bit of a nightmare. To have to worry about safety and trust during every waking moment had to be exhausting, and it showed. I was struck by the unhappiness of everyone around me. Everything seemed contrived, like a presentation. From the drive through the gates to the meeting with the client, nothing felt genuinely human.

This idea translated into the reading. Though I'm limited in what I can say about it, I realized very quickly that you can only own so much stuff before that stuff ends up owning you. Money and things had created problems every step of the way for the person I read, and I was in the surreal place of wishing they weren't in a position of such opulence. I felt bad for their wealth. If they'd been born under more normal circumstances, a happy shot at life would have been a lot more likely.

By most people's standards, my client was successful. Yet I left the experience with a visceral understanding that it was a golden-plated prison. Living in fear because of your money makes it a burden. Never truly being confident about other people's intentions in your life can lead to distrust and paranoia. An excess of money bought problems everyday people couldn't afford. The higher peaks one reaches, the more room one has to fall. Being on top of the world wasn't all it's cracked up to be.

I flew back to the US with a newfound appreciation for my life. I knew I was lucky, but it was a reality check to prioritize what I wanted out of my own success. Money didn't define happiness, it only lent an opportunity to do more, to have more, and to make more. More isn't always better. Sometimes, as the saying goes, less really is more. People strive for material success, while often neglecting their spiritual fulfillment. A life based in materialism makes people feel hollow and lack purpose. The other side emphasizes living meaningfully through the circumstances we're born into. When we know what's worth cultivating, we can grow more meaning into our lives. These aspects don't cost money; they cost time, energy, and focus. Yet the rewards these gifts give back transcend material gain. We don't take stuff with us, but we do take our consciousness. What we do with it while we're here is all that matters in the grand scheme.

A few years prior to my reading in Europe, I did a reading in my hometown of Hanford, California, for a family of immigrant farm workers. There were fourteen members of the family, and they all lived in a two-bedroom home beside a dairy on the outskirts of town.

When I came to their home, I was humbled by their hospitality. Though none of them spoke English fluently, they had a friend who took the role of interpreter throughout the reading. We sat in the cramped living room with fourteen family members and a shrine dedicated to the Virgin Mary in the middle. I could feel the love for each other in the room. It transcended language. The mother and father of the family sat cross-legged in front of me, holding each other's hands in excited anticipation for who I was going to connect with.

The children all listened respectfully as the older kids helped feed and change two newborn babies. As a group, the family relied on each other for everything. If one person had a problem, everyone intervened to help. This selflessness made it evident how close they were, and how much they prioritized each other's needs over their own comfort.

In our reading, I communicated with a young man in the family who'd been killed during an accident at work. When he came through, he reflected on the fact that his life had more meaning in twenty-two years than most people found in their entire lives. He had people to love, and his family loved him. His life was well lived because he took the opportunities to express his love when he had the chance.

I was taken aback by how *little* of a transformation this young man had made since his life review. He was filled with gratitude in life, and carried that same appreciation in death. Though the nature of his passing was violent and tragic, he died knowing that he lived well. His conscience was clear, and throughout his short life his priorities revolved around extending compassion to others.

This knowingness made acceptance and peace easier to obtain. He didn't have to go through all of the work of complicated opportunities that were never taken. He seized every chance to love. His family's humble circumstances didn't prevent them from being truly happy. My time with them was a reminder of what really matters. In many ways, they had more wealth in their quality of life than quantity of material objects. We all should strive to find balance in how we define success, recognizing the importance of making a living and the fact that money only buys us so much. Love is the currency of the soul.

Much of our time on Earth is spent undoing the barriers that prevent us from giving and receiving love. Fear, doubt, and apathy keep us stuck. Many of these barriers become ingrained in our consciousness during childhood. Though every person needs support and a nurturing presence, not everyone finds that in their parents. I was lucky to have two parents who were willing to listen and learn as I got older. They put their love for me before any technicality or obstacle. To be true to who I was, I had to risk rejection from the two guiding forces in my life. Thankfully, they were the foundation I was able to build a successful life upon. If it weren't for their constant encouragement, I wouldn't have been able to turn my ability into a gift.

Because my mom is such an advocate in my life, I wanted to ask her thoughts on how to nurture purpose in a child's life. Her support was the greatest act of love I'd ever received, and her words can benefit any parent who wonders how to do better by their child. Her excerpt reads:

> No one expects to have a medium for a child. When I was pregnant with Tyler and the time came to name him, I wanted a name that'd look good on an office door someday. Tyler Henry, Attorney at Law, had a nice ring to it. Maybe my only son would go on to become a baseball player or a doctor. That'd be a first in the family! No matter what Tyler chose to do with his life, all that mattered to me was that he was a good, kind person. I knew that with the love and support my husband could give him, he could build toward anything he set his mind towards.
>
> I just had no idea his mind was set towards being a medium! That was, until he told me of my

mother-in-law's death shortly before it happened. This initiated a long string of experiences that would regularly blow my mind. There were times when Tyler would come home from school and say that he read other students and shared shocking and accurate details about their lives. Sometimes, he even told me he "read" his teachers. At least he was reading, I thought.

I didn't know what to make of all of what he said and did. I knew he wasn't mentally ill, and he had excellent grades. He wasn't making up what he said he saw, because other people verified it. Still, I was hesitant to embrace his ability right away. I knew how mean the world was, and how important it was to keep him safe as his mother. Yet nothing I could do dissuaded him from being absolutely fascinated with religion, spirituality, and the paranormal.

Even before Tyler's initial premonition at ten years old, he was obsessed with anything related to ghosts. For a while, I assumed his medium abilities were the result of his passion for the unknown. But it ends up that his passion for the unknown was actually motivated by his ability as a medium.

As a child he seemed to know why he was here. He didn't let other people get in the way of his interests, and he didn't mind if kids judged him for it. There were many times when I'd visit his school and I'd see him on the playground, alone. At the time, it was devastating to see these moments where it was evident he didn't fit in. I wanted him to be prepared for life, and yet he marched to his own beat unapologetically. There was little I could do about it. Being an only child, he was always more interested in adults than other kids. Honoring him meant honoring that fact, and as much as I wanted to see him be social, I couldn't change him.

When Tyler reached his teenage years, it was clear his ability was only strengthening. He'd read people that we crossed paths with while running errands in our tight-knit community. I'd see someone I'd gone to school with and knew a bit about, and Tyler would read them from a distance and tell me what he sensed. He was always uncannily accurate. Whether it was sharing information about who exactly they lost, or the circumstances of the death, he always said it with total confidence. Yet for as developed as his ability was becoming, his social skills needed some help. I used to tell him that he needed to make friends or else he'd never make it socially in the real world.

It's important for children to have a healthy balance in their inner and outer worlds, but Tyler truly never got joy from being around kids his age. He knew that he was different and destined for a different life.

While his ability was kept secret from his dad until he was sixteen, I knew of his secret from the beginning. I didn't want to tell my husband because I didn't feel it was my place. Tyler would share that with him when he was ready, and I was only introduced to his skillset when he shared a premonition with me. My husband's family was conservative and unfamiliar with what a medium even was, so I assumed it was best to keep it quiet until we couldn't anymore.

In hindsight, I wish we would have been up-front about what made Tyler different. There were years that Tyler and his father had together that could have been enhanced if they really knew each other. Tyler felt like he had to withhold who he was from my husband, and as a result, my husband didn't have a fair chance to grow and evolve.

This experience taught me the importance of saying it now. When we can put ego aside and have much-needed conversations, we're one step closer to being on the same page. We may never "get" everything about one another, but that's not the point. The point is that love is shown in the effort that's put in. The more we strive to know each other, and ourselves, the more opportunities for love become apparent.

We reached that point. People were coming to our front door leaving letters and requesting readings. People obtained our phone number and would call the house at all hours of the day, looking for my son. It was obvious that word was getting out about his talent, and there was nothing I could do about it.

I had to surrender to what I couldn't control. I knew living life as a public medium could present complicated issues that I had no ability to guide him through. I didn't know much about psychics or mediums myself, but I did know the nature of the world we live in. People are cruel. While I was afraid for my son, I had to ultimately support him or risk being closed off from an important part of his authenticity.

His medium ability, his calling, was just as much of a part of him as his eye color. There was nothing that could be done to change who he was or what he felt destined to do. There were easier routes, sure, but he refused to take them. He displayed courage in being honest with me about who he was, as well as with every person he helped with his gift. When it came time for his dad to know, it took a lot of explaining and demonstrating to get him to understand.

As parents, when we know better, we should strive to do better. Believing in your child is a gift that supersedes material things. The support of a parent is invaluable. When a child looks to you for support, you're fulfilling your purpose as they're figuring out theirs. Every parent has the opportunity to lead by example, and to always strive to do better. Raising Tyler required patience and a willingness to see things in a different way. In applying both, I became a better parent and a better person.

No mother knows it all. It certainly doesn't come with a handbook. But ultimately, an inch of belief in your child will get you further than a foot of lecturing. We are who we are, and it is the diversity that differences bring to the table that make for a well-rounded world. If none of our differences were cultivated and supported, the world would be a boring place.

Ultimately, raising a child as unique as mine showed me how vital it is to surrender sometimes. I had to navigate my protective instinct and still honor who he was, trusting that he knew himself enough to know what he felt called to do. I had to apply support when he needed me, while simultaneously easing up when he needed to learn something himself. This balancing act is one all parents can relate to, and one that can be hard to manage gracefully. I realized that the traits he was worried about being ostracized for were the very traits that lent him strength. They made him who he was. To deny that was to deny his individuality.

As a parent, I had a responsibility to lift my child up, not tear him down. I didn't understand him, but it wasn't my job to understand him. My job was to act as a foundation that he could build a strong self-image on. I needed to be a shoulder to cry on, a source of support, and an undying advocate. Every child needs an advocate. Advocating for my child's authenticity made me a more authentic parent in return. I developed a more purposeful relationship with him when he knew he could be true to who he was. When we're authentically ourselves, it inspires others to do the same. If there's any message I could have for parents, it's to be the advocate for your child that you needed when you were growing up. Be the voice that you never heard, give the hugs you never got. A parent is more than a role, it's an extension of our purpose that can make ripples in the world.

I've been lucky to have my mother with me on every step of my journey. She travels the world with me and has driven me to readings on my show many times. Sometimes, she even gets to meet notable clients that I read. One such example happened when I met with Bobby Brown, the husband of the late great Whitney Houston. This reading gave an insightful look into the role of authenticity, from the most unexpected place.

When Whitney Houston came through, I was struck in hindsight by how normal her presence was. She communicated her cause of passing and a number of validating details that were only known between her and Bobby. Her energy seemed very protective of her private life and she was distinctly aware of how her family was affected by it.

She was one of the greatest pop stars the world has ever seen, revolutionizing music and gracing our screens. Yet when she came through to her living husband, her priorities weren't on any of that. At no point in our reading did she acknowledge performing, her job, or being a celebrity. Everything she valued on the other side was regarding the bonds she made in life. The love she shared with her family, and others, was the priority.

Despite making an impact on world culture many times over, she didn't once acknowledge record sales or performances. Her soul appeared to find more purpose in the moments of love that were exchanged and reciprocated, over any material accomplishments.

I was taken aback by how someone so prolific seemed so lax about her achievements. It was as if what brought her acclaim merely set the stage for other more meaningful lessons to play out. She recognized her role as a mother, a daughter, and a wife. She saw the purpose she created interpersonally and saw how that lived on through the people she loved. She communicated that she found more purpose in the "normal," sentimental moments than the extraordinary ones on stage. Life for Whitney was one performance after another, and her spirit seemed to embrace moments of normalcy over all else.

What we attribute purpose to says a lot about the lessons we learn. Many would attribute purpose to being a worldwide sensation, but true validation only came from the bonds that were mutually shared. She knew she was loved, and appreciated that, but it didn't change the hurdles she had to overcome. She was only able to overcome her struggles through the purposeful love she created with those closest to her.

In the afterlife, she was at peace. She remembered

holding her daughter's hand and going for a walk as much as she remembered breaking records. Those little human moments weren't so little, and gave insight into the human condition. No matter how ordinary or extraordinary our lives, it's the love that we take with us.

Authenticity directly connects with what we find purpose in. The activities that make us feel in alignment with our purpose are authentic to us. As we've seen, following this call takes courage and resilience. No matter who they are or what their circumstances, everybody must struggle in their environment to follow their purpose. In a world full of resistance and distraction, purposeful living can fall on the back burner. We must use external pressures as momentum to reinforce who we are. You can let your outside circumstances define you, or you can define how you respond to them. Either way, stress isn't going anywhere, so one must learn how to make diamonds from the pressure.

Before you can make authentic actions, you have to be able to know yourself enough to know your wants and needs. The more you're aware of your internal motivations and hang-ups, the more you can untangle your ego and get to the core of what you want. You may know what you want, but not how to get there. Intuition can act as that guide for discernment in helping us apply ourselves. When we know what we feel called to do, we step into who we're meant to become.

Often, intuition guides us down unexpected routes of purpose. I met with a man who was a longtime academic; he was in the process of getting his Ph.D. and had dedicated his life to studying neuroscience. He lived in California, but as a boy had always dreamt of moving to Massachusetts. This was odd, he acknowledged, because he had no family there. There was no seemingly logical reason why he'd be drawn to this place.

When we met, he was at a crossroads. He was just about ready to complete his Ph.D. program, and his personal life had suffered the toll of years' worth of grinding. He made his life revolve around his studies, and felt that in doing such he'd get closer to his purpose. Yet he had few friends, no love life, and was cripplingly lonely. As his studies went on, he began to seriously wonder if a certificate was worth the cost of his social life. He'd have the career he always dreamt of, but no one to come home to at night and share it with.

In our reading, I told him that I didn't see the trajectory of his future looking particularly bright. He had burnt himself out mentally and emotionally, and though he'd be getting his coveted degree, it wouldn't lead to happiness. I was confused as to why he seemed to be intuitively pulled to do two very different things. One intuitive thought had stayed with him from childhood, while the other motivated him to stay in school. How would the two be reconciled?

Fast forward a few months after our meeting, my client flew to a medical conference in Massachusetts, where he visited for the first time. While he was there, he hopped on an online dating service and was struck by the first photo that came up. A blond-haired woman only a year younger than him, she lived in Boston and worked as a dog trainer.

Long story short, he went on a date with this woman while in town for his conference. The meeting absolutely changed his life. He fell head over heels in love with her, and she with him. It was painful to go back to California without her. As the days turned to weeks, he began making some admittedly risky decisions. He was willing to move across the country for someone he had just met, and he couldn't explain why. He just knew it was right.

And so, he did. He didn't complete his Ph.D. program, and instead moved to Boston to be with his girlfriend and train dogs. I spoke to him recently, and we were stunned to both realize that it had been nine years since we spoke. He realized that if he hadn't gone through the Ph.D. program, he would have never needed to go to the conference where he met his future wife. In some sense, his obsession with academic pursuits wasn't in vain—it brought him to a destination he couldn't imagine in the beginning. It all worked out when he followed what he felt called to do. He was able to integrate his childhood calling to Boston with his academic pursuits as an adult, and through both found greater happiness. This acts as a representation of what we can all strive to do: honor different parts of ourselves and what we want to achieve. Through trusting our intuition and putting it into action, we help these different parts of ourselves build a brighter future. The key is being able to recognize what we truly feel called to do in the first place.

Our pursuit of our own purposefulness can be a frustrating endeavor. So many people wish they knew why they were here, but don't make the effort to understand their strengths and go with their intuition. The purposeless person looks to others for instruction on how to live their life. Purpose breathes life into everything we do, solidifying and manifesting that which all starts on an internal level. In life, you can be the product of your own hard work, or you can be the product of someone else's.

It can be easy to feel like finding a sense of purpose is a maddening task. It requires a fine balance of confidence and self-assurance, as well as a willingness to listen and take chances. It's important for the reader to not become obsessed with trying to identify purpose; let it be what it is. It already exists inside you.

By living more mindfully and, as a result, intuitively, we can follow those hunches that pull back the curtain on our purpose. We mustn't burn ourselves out spinning our wheels to determine why we're here. If anything, we must put ourselves out on the playing field, always trying new things and giving the Universe an opportunity to move through us. When we take the initiative, things begin to fall into place. The person who is out on the field finding their purpose gets further than the person on the sidelines trying to figure it all out. You don't have to have it figured out. None of us do. What you must be aware of is your own capabilities for greatness. You have to truly be aware of your potential. You must unblock the conditioning that tells you of a certain unfixable limitation. Everything can be resolved with enough ingenuity, patience, and application of intuition.

In conclusion, we have more than one purpose. We extract purpose from that which is authentic to ourselves. Finding purpose is a lifestyle, not an action. It becomes a lifestyle when we can become attuned to intuition, meaning, and opportunities. While some people are able to live more authentically than others, everyone brings unique strengths to the table that the world can benefit from. The world can only know you if you know yourself, though. This introspective journey isn't an easy one, and mindfulness makes the process more deliberate and meaningful. When we live authentically, we're recognizing the spirit inside of us. Authentic living supersedes our ego and represents the core nature of who we are and what we're destined to do.

Our conditioning can ultimately bring us closer, or further, to identifying purpose. Whatever we tell ourselves we can or cannot do generally proves to be correct. We self-fulfill the prophecies we make for ourselves. Ultimately, you're only as capable as you believe you are. Intuition reminds us to see past our own view of things and to consider possibilities that defy logic.

This allows for new concepts and ideas to be introduced that can have positive consequences. Our ego can recognize what gives us purpose, and living purposefully doesn't destroy ego. When we can create an ego framework that inspires us to take action, show courage, and display strength, then an adversary becomes a friend. Your ego is not the enemy to purpose, and in fact, it can harness it.

You can make great change in the world simply by being yourself. All of the great minds listed in this chapter that followed their intuition and met the call were just living their lives.

Yet, their lives were for more than just themselves. The life of Martin Luther King, Jr., went on to change the lives of every person born after him. Isaac Newton's discoveries went on to inspire discoveries for hundreds of years to come. When we know ourselves enough to seize opportunities that are right for us, mountains move.

When we live purposefully, it inspires purpose in other people. Every iconic individual to ever make great change saw a purpose for what they did. Even if it wasn't clear at the time what they would go on to accomplish, they did it anyway. They met the call with an answer. All of this requires us to face our fears and look at our innermost vulnerabilities. When you can know yourself, you're better equipped to know what you're working with.

Success is something we all strive for, be it professional

or interpersonal. Spirits on the other side relay the importance of viewing success in terms of the love we accrue. All that our souls value exists in the experiential moments in which we rose to the occasion to do better. No matter how opulent or humble our settings may be, it's the actions we put forward that define our success.

Living authentically makes us happier, healthier, and more capable of seizing the moment. When we're in alignment with who we are, we make choices that better our future selves. Spirits have lived and died to understand this lesson, and we can glean the insight they've gained. If the departed could do it over, they very often acknowledge that they'd have taken more risks in the name of authenticity. At the end of the day, who we are is all there really is. We must live with ourselves and the extent that we're willing to embrace our true nature. By being true to who you are, you give the world a light it didn't have before you. The world can only see what you have to offer when you know it yourself. Herein lies the key to authenticity: know yourself.

5

Navigate the Inevitability of Loss

The Highs and the Lows

*"No one ever told me that grief felt
so much like fear."*

—*C. S. Lewis*

Dying is an uncomfortable inevitability. Even with my understanding of an afterlife, I'm in no rush to get there. Every one of us is touched by the change death initiates, and it's never comfortable.

There's a pressure in certain spiritual circles to live life in a perpetual state of contentedness. Surely, if someone is really living spiritually, they'll have the tools to deal with any loss that may come their way, right?

Wrong. Loss blindsides us. Grief is an overwhelming emotional journey that begins and never seems to end. We carry the losses we experience throughout our entire lives. Our attitudes around loss influence our ego's view of it, but we're not immune to feeling. No matter how we choose to frame unexpected setbacks, they still hurt.

Honoring this pain is essential to being truthful with yourself. Every single one of us is molded and shaped by the losses we experience, depending on when and how they happen to us. Our views on mortality and how we cope with it can tremendously affect our ability to move forward. In this chapter, I'll cover my experience with the highs and the lows and what the departed can teach us about navigating the Here.

For all the amount of loss that I've witnessed first-hand, I've been surprised by the resilience of the human spirit. Love is a powerful force in the face of grief. What we do with that grief is also a testament to the power we have over it.

I don't want to wrongly give the impression that love is a cure-all for all that ails us. Love doesn't pay the bills or bring a departed loved one back into the physical world. I've found, however, that when navigating grief, coming from a loving place can help. Showing yourself love and compassion facilitates healing. Honoring those in your life that have lived and died is an implicitly loving action. Love is a catalyst for purpose and greater meaning.

There are a multitude of ways we experience loss. Each can be approached more mindfully to make the process a little less painful. It's important to not just view grief as something people experience when a loved one dies. Grief is felt over a number of losses. Occupational or financial loss is something most people experience at one time or another. The end of a close friendship or a moment when we felt betrayed can leave a crater in our emotional well-being. Even our expectations of how things should be can lead to grief when things don't go our way. Life is full of many little deaths.

How we move through life's continual losses defines our resilience. Our ability to accept what we cannot control plays a huge part in our inner worlds. Nobody likes the thought of loss, but some people struggle deeply at even the smallest of letdowns. Expectations lead to disappointment. It's impossible to not have expectations in life, but we should ask ourselves if our expectations are doing more harm than good. While expectations can help us work harder and externalize what we want, they can also have control over us. Balance is key.

Life doesn't happen to you; it happens through you. Change kicks up the dust so that new behavior can settle. No matter how painful your experiences, what you do with it all leaves a legacy greater than the pain itself. When pain is repressed, it wreaks havoc on our unconscious and can lead to generational trauma, even if we think we're past it. If we aren't able to work on ourselves, our children of the future will have to take up where we left off. This is the nature of family cycles.

Grief has always been something to navigate. So much so that you've probably heard about the stages of grief, and how we all go through different steps to acceptance. In recent years, the idea of universal stages of grief has been thoroughly debunked. Proponents of this idea can't agree on whether there's five stages of grief or twelve. This lack of consistency reflects a greater truth: grief is unique to the experiencer.

Yes, there're aspects of denial with any loss. There's also anger, bargaining, depression, and acceptance about various things at various times. However, your journey through grief is not like a series of stops at a train station. Denial isn't necessarily the first step, nor is acceptance the last.

When it comes to closure, I always emphasize that readings aren't a cure for grief. They validate that consciousness transcends physical death, but aren't a cure-all to the natural grief process. Closure implies a period when it's really a comma. We can have moments where we make progress in making amends with our grief, but it's always there in some form. Readings can facilitate progress and remind people that their loved ones exist in a different form. Even with this knowingness, we have to honor physical loss and the grief it causes us. To deny this is to deny being human.

Many think of loss as something we have to move past. I view loss as something that forever changes any life it touches, and expecting ourselves to move on entirely can do more harm than good. The grief stages are nice in theory; they provide a beginning, a middle, and an end. But the true nature of grief is carried with us throughout our entire lives. Years may pass, and grief still may flare up or rear its head in a painful way. Grief can be baffling, frustrating, and inconsistent. We can take two steps forward and five steps back. It's not a clear-cut series of stages that we graduate from.

I emphasize this because I think it's important to set realistic goals. We shouldn't aim to overrule our grief. We should strive to integrate it. When we can view grief as something that we shouldn't try to get rid of, it helps our cause. Honor your grief. Recognize the emotions physical absence has stirred. Only then can you do something transformative with it.

One of the most profound readings I ever did was with someone who was facing their own impending death. This story changed how I view grief itself and lends credence to the idea that we can make something beautiful from the inevitable.

The reading was with a woman named Heather. At that time, Heather was in her mid-thirties, happily married, and had a seven-year-old little boy. She'd seen me on television in early episodes and was determined to get in touch. Only recently had she been given a life-changing diagnosis: stage 4 terminal cancer. Time was of the essence.

After we set up the appointment, I expected to show up to a solemn scene. But as my manager drove me up to a suburb outside of LA, I met a smiling woman who greeted me with an enthusiastic hug. I was taken aback by her positivity, her radiance, and how very present she seemed. As we went through her front archway, I saw photographs of her and her young son greeting me at the door. It was clear how much love she and her family shared.

I could see the exhaustion on Heather's face, yet as we began the reading, she kept smiling. I could tell that she was being strong for me so as to not show any of the pain she was in. I thought about how she'd probably gotten used to doing that for her son, her husband, and everyone else who loved her.

In that moment, it was hard to focus. I wished more than anything that I had the power to stop this woman from dying; it was one of the rare moments where I felt true frustration with the Universe. It didn't seem one bit fair. I knew of the peace that awaited her in death, but that didn't stop my awareness of the inevitable anguish her family would feel from her physical absence.

I tried my best to work through what I was feeling, as any emotions of my own are a hindrance to the quality of a reading. As I centered myself, I immediately brought through Heather's extended family. They came through with names, dates, and specific memories that made Heather smile from ear to ear. Their inside jokes and childhood references reminded her of times when she wasn't sick, and gave her comfort in knowing that those she loved would be waiting for her when it was her time to go.

They communicated an inherently important message to Heather: make the best of the time she had and navigate the inevitability of her physical loss. The departed encouraged her to make use of the time she had left by communicating everything she could to those she held close to her. By ensuring nothing went unsaid to those who meant the most, Heather knew she'd be able to transition a little more peacefully.

She did this by saying all there was to say in the present moment—she didn't wait.

Heather recorded our reading for her family to be able to watch long after she'd transitioned, so they'd find comfort in the same validations she received during our reading. She created a time capsule filled with handwritten letters and knickknacks to be opened decades later. She recorded a video that was to be played during her funeral, thanking each person she knew would show up. Most profoundly, she even filled out birthday cards for her son to open every birthday of his from seven to forty years old.

After our reading, I asked Heather what had changed most since getting her diagnosis. She told me that since receiving the news, she found herself being a lot more present. Even more meaningfully, she said that any time she was with her son, she never once picked up her phone. She realized the importance of that time with him, for both of them. This was a vital lesson we can all learn from, no matter what we're going through: strive to be as present as we can with ourselves and with those we love. Just because we're physically present doesn't mean we're mentally present; being mindful of where our energy is going helps us dedicate it to what really matters.

Heather made the most of the limited time she had left. While she could have easily been petrified in fear, she embraced what she couldn't control. She made a legacy for herself while she was still alive. I left my time with Heather with an extreme awareness of the importance of seizing the little moments. The little stuff is the big stuff in the end.

I've found through my work that how people cope with death often brings out traits that reflect what they value in life. Though we all know we will die someday, receiving the news of a limited lifespan immediately changes perspective. All the planning we do in our lives, and the work we do to secure those plans, suddenly comes to a halt. Planning for a decade in the future is useless when you have six months to live, and how people deal with this can teach us a lot about what really matters in life.

One example of this took place with an elderly client named George, who had just been diagnosed with a terminal illness. After years of not going to a doctor at all, he was driven to the ER when a neighbor found him unconscious in his home, where he lived alone. No family visited him, and for good reason. By his own admission, he had been a ragingly mean alcoholic and was abusive to every member of his family.

When he received the news from his doctor that his lapse into unconsciousness was indicative of his nervous system beginning to decline, no one was there to comfort him. Yet as horrible as it was to receive this news, George said he suddenly felt sobered by it.

He had long put off rekindling his relationship with his son, assuming his son would eventually reach out when he'd recovered from his father's antics. George was admittedly cruel to his ex-wife, and had never apologized to her. Yet in hearing the worst news of his life, he was suddenly motivated to do what he had put off for years: take accountability for the hurt he'd caused. Time was of the essence.

He always knew how his actions were impacting his family. Even when he couldn't find empathy for them because of his altered state of mind, he knew the pain he caused. Only on that life-changing day did he make a conscious effort to finally validate the feelings of the people he loved.

After a lot of thought, he wrote his ex-wife a series of letters taking accountability for all his wrongdoing during their relationship. He explained what he wished he had done differently and how he understood the pain he'd caused her, and apologized for everything. He also rekindled his relationship with his estranged son.

But the news that he was going to die didn't only change how George went about his human relationships. He withdrew the savings he'd tirelessly scrabbled for over decades and went on a vacation—his first in over twenty years!

George had never been a giving person before, but things were radically different now. Previously opposed to having animals in his house, George adopted a Labrador puppy a few months into his progressive decline. They were inseparable.

When we met, George told me he wanted, more than anything, to keep living the life he'd finally created for himself—at the very end of his time on Earth. He was conflicted by the fact that the happiest time of his life had only been sparked by his impending death. He realized how differently his life could have unfolded if he'd only learned to show empathy, for both the people he loved and for himself. He lived more meaningfully in his last days than he had years prior. He realized the importance of experiences, not things.

My time with both Heather and George reflected an inevitable truth we will all face: one day, we're going to die. It's what we do with the time that we have between now and then that makes up the quality of our lives. Both had to face their mortality head-on, and made something positive from the worst of circumstances. We don't need the news of a terminal illness to start living more mindfully. We owe it to those who have, and ourselves, to make the most of our time.

As human beings, we have to reckon with our own death and the deaths of others. Both provide unique opportunities to apply mindfulness and do something meaningful. Our ego tends to be uncomfortable with change, and death is the greatest initiator of change that there is. It's hard to let go. If it were easy, what was held onto would be meaningless.

Accepting the harshities of life is important if they cannot be changed. We can mull over whether we could have said or done something differently or beat ourselves up about how things should have gone. When we can see things as they are, not how we want them to be, we have more room to heal. We must be real with ourselves, and not feel pressure to "get over it." No matter how spiritual or religious we are, pain hurts. To expect a quick fix only leads to more disappointment. We must strive to grow where we're planted.

One of the greatest tools we have is our ability to create a legacy from our loss. We can't undo the fact that someone died. But we have power in what we do to honor their life and to create something that helps fill that gap. Think of the person you've lost. Though you'll never be able to introduce them to future friends and family, you can uphold their memory and what they valued. I often emphasize the importance of introducing our departed loved ones to the world through our actions. Take what can be gleaned from your loved one's life, what they represented, and what they valued. Just because they're no longer here physically doesn't mean those qualities can't be continued and live on. Approaching our grief this way can have incredible effects on our morale and our feeling of connection to them on the other side.

This idea was exemplified in a reading I did during a live show. I was in Dallas, Texas, reading an audience of over three thousand people. Immediately I felt pulled to the very back of auditorium, where the stage's lights didn't even effectively reach. The person I had a message for sat in the darkness, and I could tell that this was a son coming through.

As I connected more with this spirit, I was taken aback by his exuberance. He was only a few years older than me at the time that he died. He communicated an insistence and an excitement to talk to his mother.

When I found her, she wasn't expecting a reading. She didn't think that where she was seated would allow for a reading, but it did. When she stood up to the microphone, I relayed her son's temperament and how he died. All was going accordingly when I was interrupted by a strange message, "Because I died, other people lived."

I wasn't sure how to deliver this. I didn't want to say such a thing if it was a misinterpretation; after all, it didn't seem to make much sense. He was communicating excitedly and was insistent that I share this fact with his mother. To him, it was one of the greatest achievements his soul had acquired, and he wasn't even alive physically to witness it.

As I relayed this information, his mother was stunned. He further communicated that he had died in a vehicular accident while drunk driving. When his mother received the news, she felt like her life had ended in that moment. Somehow though, she went on to honor her pain through activism. She created a drunk driving awareness charity that went to local high schools and colleges emphasizing the importance of sober driving. Through the activism her son's death inspired, she was able bring awareness of the subject to individuals who wouldn't have otherwise been made aware.

In her son's life review, he realized that his death led to lives being saved, but only because of how his mother handled her loss. He saw firsthand that there were a number of students who had heard of his story and, as a result, took drunk driving more seriously. All it took was awareness to prevent some individuals from making poor choices. This awareness wouldn't have come from the source that it did if the woman I read hadn't lost a son.

Through his death, countless young lives were saved from the same fate. As I communicated with this woman and her son, he was overjoyed by what she went on to do. His life had more meaning, and his death wasn't in vain, because it prevented others from the same fate. This wouldn't have been possible if his mother hadn't displayed the strength that she had. By creating a legacy for her son, she prevented future mothers from having to experience the pain she was in. This was empowering to her son's soul, and soothed hers in the process. Through the creation of something greater than loss, both were able to find greater peace along the way.

Honoring our grief transforms it. Not everyone will feel called to do the same things with their grief, and the variety of opportunities it allows for are endless. While the woman at my Dallas show brought worldly awareness to how her son died, many feel more comfortable preserving how someone lived. This, too, can be incredibly empowering.

I've seen countless creative ways people have done this. One client I read recently lost her father when she was nine months pregnant. She took her dad's favorite plaid shirt and turned it into a teddy bear for her newborn daughter to hold on to. This little gesture acted as a reminder for her and her daughter that his influence lived on. Every time she saw that teddy bear, she thought of him. It was a conversation piece in the family, and they'd often have it out on display during the holidays. This little remembrance made her father's spirit exceedingly happy. He was still a part of the fun.

I've also seen gestures go on to inspire the course of people's lives. One client's mother was a voracious baker. When her mom died, she saved all of the baking tins, whisks, and cutlery that her mother always used. Her own daughter then went on to find a passion for cooking which was spurred by the usage of these objects in her childhood. By preserving what her mother enjoyed and sharing it with members of the family, she made her influence continue on in an unexpected way.

Finally, honoring the legacy of how someone lived can change the lives of others. I read a woman whose husband died when their son was only a year old. Her husband was in school to become an entomologist, which involved studying bugs and bringing back specimens from faraway countries. On a work trip to Brazil, her husband was killed in a botched robbery and she was left to raise her son alone.

In raising her son, she had an incredibly difficult time discussing the departed husband and father they lost. She removed photographs of them together from the house and took away reminders that made the grief too painful. The butterfly specimens he had encased in glass were put in boxes and shoved into the attic. In some ways, the extent of her grief made her husband a ghost that wasn't talked about.

That is, until her son was seven years old. One day, he was going through some boxes and found one of the butterflies encased in glass. When he asked his mother where it came from, she admitted that it was his father's and suggested he put it back. But he didn't. Her son took the specimens out of the box and insisted hanging them in his room. This began his lifelong love for bugs and insect preservation. Ultimately, her son would grow up to become a leading entomologist, fulfilling the very career his father died pursuing.

Her son's willingness to honor his father's passions

transformed his life. Though she wasn't comfortable bringing reminders of grief to light, her son took a different approach when he was given the opportunity. We owe it to those we love to introduce them to those they'll never meet physically, through our actions. When we can preserve what meant most to them and share it with the world, we keep their lives going in our own way.

As a medium, I've learned that funerals and memorials are more for the living to have an opportunity to grieve, than for the departed. When we die, we don't care about what happens to our body or where it goes. They view their former bodies like we do vehicles, and death is merely the impound lot. Meanwhile, the passenger of the car is alive and well and, if anything, has upgraded to a new means of transportation.

Funerals allow for us to meet with others, remember someone's life, and begin processing our own grief. The departed encourage us to mourn, as it's only natural. But the true nature of the grief process sets in weeks, months, and years after we say goodbye ceremonially. So, too, do our opportunities to honor them.

Since writing my last book, I experienced the loss of someone dear to me. I was faced with the choice of how I wanted to remember him, and I handled it in a bit of a unique way. My manager Ron Scott discovered me when I was only a teenager, and was a catalyst for my career. He always believed in me and was endlessly supportive. Ron was in his seventies, had no immediate family, and took the role of a grandfather in my life.

In the eighties, Ron was a hotshot publicist for some of the biggest names in Hollywood. John Stamos, *MacGyver*'s Richard Dean Anderson, and a number of big hair bands were all represented by Ron. When we met, his career had slowed down and he represented mostly up-and-coming entertainers.

To know Ron was to love him. Inside his apartment in West Hollywood, my picture sat framed near his entryway before I'd ever even "made it." He saw a future for me that I didn't even see for myself. He was a very unconventional man who was known for his love of going to lunch with friends, and his booming laughter. He was incredibly campy and hilariously flamboyant, always prepared with a witty one-liner. He knew classic film star Mae West well, and in many ways embodied her attitude and sense of humor.

The last time I saw Ron alive, I knew it would be the last time we'd see one another. I had just left a meeting at NBC Universal with the E! network, and Ron pulled up in a newly purchased convertible. With wispy gray hair flying in the wind, he had the biggest smile on his face as he drove away. For all the success he had in the eighties, he finally was getting the recognition he deserved in his last years.

When I received the news that Ron had died, I was numb. I knew he had poor health, and I always could intuitively tell when he wasn't taking his blood pressure medicine. I'd scold him in a hilarious role reversal, and he'd promise half-heartedly to take it. He knew there were deeper issues than heart troubles brewing, though. Ron had stomach cancer and didn't want to ruin the mood with his diagnosis. He was dedicated to having a good time and didn't see the need for people to feel bad for him. "That's show business!" he'd always say at the funniest of times.

Shortly after Ron passed, I was invited to his memorial. Being that I was the only client he represented at the end of his life, his friends expected me to come and prepare a speech. I knew that unless his funeral was a costume party, Ron wouldn't have wanted hoopla around his death. If a muscular man wasn't going to pop out of a cake to the bemusement of his audience, Ron wouldn't have been interested.

So, I didn't go to my own manager's memorial. It just didn't feel right. He spent his entire life trying to focus on everything lighthearted, and to have a send-off for him with sobbing people just didn't feel appropriate.

Instead, I went to a historic diner that he and I frequented between appointments. He'd always get a grilled cheese sandwich, and so, I did the same. Sitting there alone in the booth, I couldn't help but feel sad. I could have really used one of his one-liners in that moment. The silence was deafening.

My grief for Ron hit me in waves. More than anything, I wished I would have appreciated the moments we had together more at the time. In hindsight I yearned to learn from him, to ask him about his childhood and retain every fascinating story he experienced. I wish I'd followed up about his early experiences with Marilyn Monroe and Elvis and what life was like for a gay man in the fifties. When he died, it wasn't just a bunch of Hollywood history that died with him—he encompassed my history, too.

Ron's death put me in the same position countless people I've read were in. I had regret. I didn't know the "right" way to grieve, or what to do. I was left wishing I could receive a message of my own to know that wherever he was, he was okay. I felt desperation. In time, my grief ebbed and flowed, and some days were harder than others. Only months after his death did I begin noticing indications that his soul was still with me.

It started with his laugh. Anyone who knew him could hear his laugh from a mile away. I'd be going throughout my day and randomly have visions of his smiling face. Then, as the occurrences continued, I'd hear his familiar chuckle. It would happen at the most bizarre times, often when I was stressed or upset.

One such occurrence happened while I was filming my television show. I was asked to co-host a fashion show with Miss Universe, Alicia Machado. The theme for this event was ancient Egypt, and as I walked through the corridors of LA's City Hall, I was hit by a flurry of colors and sounds. Men dressed as nine-foot-tall sarcophaguses danced around in ornate costumes, while models walked invisible runways to practice their routines.

It was overstimulating, to say the least. To make matters more intense, I was being followed by an entire camera crew who were capturing the event for *Hollywood Medium*. After I was finished presenting, I thought the stress of the evening would be over. It was just beginning.

I was approached by a producer who said that Steve Carrell was in the building. It'd be great, they said, if I could talk to him on camera. The only catch was that none of his PR people were aware of this plan, so I had to find him and talk to him myself. Though I knew I'd have a hard time doing that alone, I had Miss Universe by my side, and who is going to say no to Alicia Machado?!

Well, Steve Carrell was suddenly on the run. After Alicia agreed to help strike up a conversation with him, we saw Steve heading into a different building. So, we chased him. It was like a scene from a movie. People in ornate garb and stilts were having to dodge us as we ran through City Hall, jumping over jury armchairs and dodging models who were getting ready for the night ahead.

Then, it happened. We finally caught up to Steve before his people did, and Alicia made the introduction. He was gracious and we talked for a few moments, until out of nowhere his people jumped out and escorted him away from us as fast as they could. Such was the nature of dealing with big celebrities. As Steve Carrell got escorted away by a handler who yelled about us not having permission to film, I heard the laugh. Ron's laugh. It was as if from the other side, he was amused by the ridiculousness of the situation and was lending a reminder: "that's show business!"

Ron's presence in my life showed me the importance of humility and humor. He always found the light in every situation. The campier and more ridiculous something was, the more he liked it. At moments in my life that would fit this bill, I was reminded of his presence in spirit. Receiving the message of his laugh was so much more than just a laugh. It was a way of him telling me to not take this journey so seriously. To be able to act as a reminder of this even in death meant that Ron's life served a purpose beyond what he could see for himself. In my grieving process, I choose to look for the moments where I can handle things more like Ron did. The legacy he created for his life transcends his seventy-four years. His legacy is a daily reminder to do better, be funnier, and go with the flow. In this way, I was able to take my own grief and transform it into a tool for living more fully. People that I meet in the future will never be able to meet Ron physically, but I can introduce him to them through how his personality changed mine. It's said that we're all made up of everyone we've ever met, and to some extent, that's true. How we choose to introduce the world to those we've loved and lost is a testament to love itself.

Loss is a universal part of the human experience. When I communicate with the other side, they appear to be very aware of the losses we experience. They refer to divorces, acknowledge job losses, and can sometimes even foretell health struggles. All of these experiences are viewed as important by those in spirit. They acknowledge that difficulties lend an opportunity to rise to the occasion and transform.

Sometimes, certain losses feel destined to lead us to greater horizons. In my life, getting rejected by one network led to being accepted by another. I couldn't exactly see that at the time, but we never can when we're in the middle of such transitional states. Hindsight allows for us to sometimes understand how setback led to opportunity. Sometimes, it's harder to find the meaning in our losses. When things are exceptionally difficult, it can be hard to see a way out. It's important to always remember that having a bad experience doesn't mean you have a bad life. Setbacks are inevitable. The resilience you show, no matter what the situation, pays off in the end. Trusting in divine timing gives us solace in unpredictable times.

Divine timing is a concept that's continually referred to during readings. Essentially, divine timing means that certain opportunities only happen when they're meant to. The phrases "the stars aligned" or Shakespeare's "star-crossed lovers" come to mind. No matter what we do to try to alter, control, or manipulate, things only fall into place when the wheel of fortune lends us our turn.

Oftentimes, divine timing requires us to lose something in order to move in a different direction. It makes room for what's yet to come by creating a void that is only to be filled later on. Loss initiates change. When we go through discomfort, we grow through it. Like putting a pot of water on a burner, only when heat is applied does change begin. Loss can act as a force of momentum that makes us look at things differently, go inward, and reach new heights.

I see examples of this regularly during readings. Every time I've met with a client whose significant other just broke up with them, I often present the question if within that rejection there exists an opportunity. Oftentimes, I'll intuit information about the person that they're destined to be with in the long term, and that person isn't the individual that just broke up with them.

I did a reading with Loni Love and intuited knowledge about her love life. I received a message that hit me insistently, and I knew it was an answer to a question coming through. I saw undoubtedly that Loni was meant to be in love with a man named "James." Everyone she had loved up until that point was leading her to him. Despite her insistence that James was a former love interest, I could tell that despite previous relationship struggles, it all happened for a greater reason. They were meant to be together, and if anything in her past had been different, it wouldn't unravel the way it was destined to.

Sure enough, it was. As of this writing, Loni is happily in a relationship with James. The absence that was created by other people lent an opportunity for the right one. If she hadn't experienced difficulties in this aspect of her life, she wouldn't have ultimately gotten what she was looking for. The waiting paid off.

The payoff from loss sometimes takes a long time to see, but it always grants a chance to glean something greater. I've done countless readings in which job losses have facilitated someone following their career passions. Sometimes we have to be unchained from obligation to fulfill the responsibilities that call out to us. We can't juggle too much at one time, and loss can sometimes free up space and energy for greater things.

One aspect of loss that's hard to be altruistic about is health issues. When we experience a blow to our health, everything else falls by the wayside. Our health is our everything. To lose it, or face the prospect of losing it, means that our lives are forever changed. Whereas in our careers we can find a new job, or in our love lives find a new partner, we only have one body. If it turns against us, that loss can be devastating.

In my recent health struggles with a collapsed lung and complications from surgery, I was faced with a new reality: nerve pain. The brain surgery I'd undergone at eighteen was nothing compared to the pain of an entirely collapsed lung. Because surgery revealed my lungs were in worse shape than they thought, the procedure went on for longer, and I was cut up in a number of places.

Pain makes you present. When you're hurting, it's incredibly difficult to focus on anything else. All I could think about post-surgery was how much pain I was in. When my pain was at my worst, I found irony in it all. It felt like the worst cause for mindfulness ever! Even if I wanted to worry about the future, I couldn't concentrate on all of that while hurting. It grounded my consciousness in a way that made me deeply aware of being in my body.

Nerve pain is difficult to treat. Living with this continual health issue has made me relinquish my control and demanded that I surrender to it. I've had to consciously work through the emotional layers of pain and do a lot of mental reframing when I'm feeling my worst. I can't change my health, I can only choose how I move forward with it. After all, our body has to last us (hopefully) eighty years minimum, and we're only given one. We may as well honor our vessel and treat it gently. We will all deal with instances of poor health if we live long enough. Being able to approach pain purposefully is a lesson on navigating what we can't control. This version of the Serenity Prayer by Reinhold Niebuhr says it best:

> *God, give me grace to accept with serenity*
> *the things that cannot be changed,*
> *Courage to change the things*
> *which should be changed,*
> *and the Wisdom to distinguish*
> *the one from the other.*

We can't escape loss in our lives, but we possess implicit power in our response. When we can distinguish between that which we can and cannot control, we live more effectively. Knowing what's worth trying to change and what's not helps us live more efficiently. When we can view loss as a void that creates space for greater change, our narrative around it shifts. We must honor our pain and grieve accordingly. In the beginning, it's important to have a mourning phase. Don't feel guilty for being devastated. It's a starting point.

Through our grief we come to a place where we eventually must rise to the occasion. It may not be right away, but the Universe presents us chances to make up for that deficit. Only through trust, intuition, and self-awareness can we seize the opportunities set before us.

One aspect of loss most of us will face is the death of a pet. I speak of this differently than the loss of a human because our relationships with our pets warrant a discussion that's nuanced differently. Yes, losing a pet can provide an opportunity to honor a legacy. However, more profoundly, the feelings of grief from the loss of a pet can teach us about ourselves.

Pets provide unconditional love, but they give us a chance to receive love, too. So many people are more comfortable with animals than humans, in part because some pets can be trusted more than people. Animals don't judge our character. Dogs yearn for companionship no matter how kindly or cruelly they're treated. Pets embody a loyalty that we seldom find in people.

When we're faced with a situation in which we have to say goodbye to our loyal companions, it can be devastating. While pets are a part of our lives, we are their whole lives. I've been made keenly aware of this through countless readings in which pets have come through. No matter what form consciousness took physically, anything with sentience continues on. If bonds can be created, that translates to the next realm of existence. I'm sure dogs, and all pets, serve a purpose existentially that factors into their spiritual journeys.

My work has made me look at the individuals in my life through a different lens. When I do a reading for someone whose mother died, I come home with a greater appreciation for my own mom. Similarly, I see this with pets. In October of 2020, I experienced an unexpected loss when my beloved maltipoo Mindi died. Seeing how often pets come through in readings, I always made it a point to appreciate Mindi's role in my life. Still, I didn't give much thought that she'd pass away under such circumstances. In hindsight, I was frustrated that I couldn't intuit my constant companion's health problems when she was in such bad shape. After she passed, I couldn't help but remember a strange synchronicity that occurred the week before she died. After months of not picking up my tarot cards, I decided on a whim to do a reading. *Something* felt important enough for me to pull out a tool I usually reserve for dire situations.

The cards generally provided more clarity in times of stress, but I didn't know what exactly I was needing to better understand. I pulled three cards, only to have a difficult time interpreting what they were trying to say. So, I pulled two more. My attempts at getting the message were in vain. Frustrated, I went into the kitchen to fix a snack with the hopes of giving the cards another shot a little later. When I walked into the living room, my cards were scattered everywhere. While I was away, Mindi managed to jump onto the table and was gnawing on three of the cards. I was irked that the dog ruined the deck and I'd need to buy another. I picked up the cards in her mouth and exclaimed, "Bad girl!" As I did, I noticed the three cards she'd destroyed actually made sense when interpreted together. It seemed to vaguely refer to receiving a message or news, alongside depression and sadness. I brushed it off and was faintly amused with myself that I'd see meaning in the cards my dog chewed up.

Looking back, I believe this really was a message from something greater. Through synchronicity, Mindi picked three cards that foretold news that would lead to great sadness. At the time, I only half-realized what was being conveyed, and should have gone with my gut more fervently. Regardless, I was faced with a tragedy that made me more mindful of the importance of never taking things for granted. Though we were only together for two and a half years, Mindi gave me love in times when I needed it most. She saw me through some of the most challenging times I've ever faced. When everybody wanted something from me, she was just happy with my company.

The loss of a pet is unavoidable. Yet it teaches us a valuable lesson about unconditional love and our ability to relish in what we have. All too often, people hold regret for not saying or doing something more before a loved one died. If we take the lessons our pets teach us and view humans as an opportunity to extend that idea, our time becomes more meaningful. Sometimes it takes loving, and being loved, unconditionally to show us what we're capable of in other circumstances.

Every relationship we have can teach us something about love. Some teach us the importance of giving love, others about receiving it. Some people teach us the importance of loving ourselves first. Whether we learn these lessons about love from people or animals, each has value in the accumulation of love we take with us. One fascinating thing about love is that it's a concept that means something different to every person, but we all know what it feels like. Some may say that love, itself, is ineffable. It's beyond words, but that's never stopped poets and lovers from trying. I've learned throughout readings that love acts as a reminder of our true spiritual nature. When we love and are loved, we are transcendant. Love taps into the part of ourselves that is here for a purpose, and nurtures that purpose.

I recently watched an interview done by renowned poet Maya Angelou. In it, she shared her thoughts on love and its role in loss. She explains her complicated relationship with her mother, and how it taught her what love truly is. At seventeen, Maya gave birth to her son and made the decision to leave her mother's fourteen-room house. She was struck by her mother's understanding, and was told she could always come home. Every time life got her down, Maya could find solace in her mother's open house and warm meals. One day, her mother told her that she was one of the greatest women she'd ever met, in league with Eleanor Roosevelt. Though Maya wasn't yet renowned as she would grow to become, her mother saw profound purpose and potential in her. Knowing that her mother believed in her and held her in such high regard made Maya wonder if her mother was indeed correct. What if she was extraordinary? This act of unconditional love and belief validated Maya, it liberated her to see the potential in herself and pursue it. As her mother neared the end of her life, Maya saw an opportunity to liberate her. She says:

> I went back to my house, and something said, "Go back." I was in my pajamas. I jumped in my car and ran, and the nurse said, "She's just gone."
> You see . . . love liberates. It doesn't bind. Love says, I love you. I love you if you're in China, I love you if you're cross town, I love you in Harlem, I love you. I would like to be near you. I'd like to have your arms around me, I'd like to hear the

voice in my ear. But that's not possible now, so I love you. Go.

Love is an act of liberation, for others and ourselves. It's all that matters in the end. We all have the ability to liberate others with our love. Equally, we must aim to create relationships in which we're liberated as well. Though we can pick our friends, we can't pick our family. Within these relationships there're often soul-lessons at work. Children take up the lessons their parents have left off on. Those of us who have loving parents must appreciate the good and learn from what could've been done better. Parent–child dynamics can be complex and evolve as we get older. Ultimately, as is the natural way, children live to inevitably watch their parents pass away. Coping with the loss of a parent can be the hardest thing we ever deal with. If we had a close relationship with our parents, their passing can feel like a guiding light has gone out. To those who face their parents' passings on more distant terms, death can seem like an abrupt end to an unresolved sentence. In both cases, the death of a parent initiates a whole lot of emotional changes that we must process and integrate.

As we've covered earlier, it's important to live a life that minimizes the chances of things going unsaid. We must know the true nature of our feelings, and validate those that we love in honor of those feelings. But what happens when we're left to cope with what was said but never resolved?

Sometimes, it's not what went unsaid that's most painful to deal with. Occasionally, a reading will reveal a situation in which the departed feel regret for something they did say and never got to explain. Death can be unexpected, and sometimes it prevents our loved ones from clarifying their true feelings when they're alive. This leaves us with a lot to have to unpack. I witnessed this very situation in my own family, and was actually able to help resolve the situation with a message from the other side.

My paternal grandfather was a hardworking family man with three sons. My dad was the youngest, and fulfilled the stereotype as the ornery little brother. Growing up in the sixties, my dad had a conservative and traditional childhood. His parents attended church and came from a long line of deeply religious people. Though my dad was conservative, he was a bit of a rebel in his youth. He was unsuccessful in getting my grandma's permission to dye his hair black as a teenager. He met my mom when they were both thirteen, and they lived together before marriage, which was a little controversial for the time. When my dad was a little older, his father was diagnosed with lung cancer. This wasn't a massive surprise, because my grandpa Henry smoked a pack a day, sometimes two. My grandfather's oncologist said it was the worst case of lung cancer he'd ever seen, and watching his father die was deeply traumatic for my dad.

Shortly after I came out of the medium closet, my

dad wanted to better understand my ability. I'd demonstrated it by going through his yearbooks and intuiting details about his former classmates, with amazing results. My dad didn't know how I could do it, but he had no doubt that I could. One day, a message came through in a strangely clairaudient way. I heard a voice say simply, "Tell Dave it's okay to not feel pressure about church."

Knowing that my dad was receptive to my abilities, I figured I'd deliver the message. And so, I did. When I told him, he confided in me something I didn't know until that point. As my grandfather was on his deathbed, in and out of consciousness, he asked something of my dad. His final request to his son was to always stay involved in church.

His dad came through to me with a message I didn't understand, but it freed my dad of a lot of conflicting feelings. My dad was never the traditional churchgoing type and went out of respect for his parents. As an adult, my uncle was excommunicated from his church, and it left a bad impression on all three siblings. Church didn't feel like a welcoming place. To have to deal with this big ask from his father was painful, and he risked feeling like he let him down in some way.

In delivering this message, I was taken aback not only by its spontaneity, but by what it meant in the big picture. Clearly, wherever my grandfather's spirit was, it had changed its mind about the importance of church. My grandfather's spirit made the realization many souls make on the other side: you don't need anything other than yourself to connect to God. It doesn't matter where you have a relationship with God, as long as you do. Grandpa Henry, whose name I continue, was an incredible man that I never got to meet in the physical world. His message to me was an introduction of sorts, and through that message he was able to resolve his final words to his son. My dad and I both left the experience feeling a sense that things had come full circle. Spiritual connection was important to my grandfather, so much so that he emphasized it in his last moments. Here we were, harnessing the gift of a spiritual ability that brought us closer together. I like to think that we accomplished what my grandpa Henry had always valued: honoring a higher power through human connection.

In conclusion, navigating the inevitability of loss is a lifelong task. Loss can leave us fretting over what went unsaid and having to cope with what was said. It's normal in any case to have regret or to wish we could have done more. I think it's naive to say that every interaction we have with a person was at its peak potential. We could have always done more, and this fact should inspire us to try to do more now. We don't know exactly when loss will present itself in our lives, but it will. The mentality we have going into it doesn't entirely shield us from its harm. We must honor our pain, mourn our loss, and then ultimately find meaning in it all. It's up to us to honor the legacy of those we love through our actions. Life presents an opportunity for us to create legacies of our own, by honoring the legacies of those that came before us. We are all connected through time and space, all different fingers on the same hand. Though the knowingness of this interconnection doesn't make physical loss easier, it lends a chance to honor the eternal spirit of those we love most.

The quote, "They say you die twice; once when you stop breathing, and the second time when your name is spoken for the last time," comes to mind. Though our souls live on, our bodies do have an expiration date. What we do with our time sets the tone for how we're remembered and how our individual role goes on to change the collective. When we carry on the memory of our loved ones through making new memories, they, too, are more fulfilled. We all have the ability to influence and change the world around us, on some small or large scale. This fact is reflected in life reviews, and makes me personally more cognizant of my actions and how they change others. No small act of kindness goes unnoticed in the end. Everything we do with our loved ones in mind enhances the lives they lived.

Grief can put us in a place that seems helpless and hopeless. It's important to acknowledge our grief and go through the mourning processes. As we've seen, there's no one way to grieve. Our loss is as unique as what we gained. After processing the initial change death brings, we have fertile ground to grow something out of all the hurt. Our loved ones on the other side emphasize the importance of keeping their memory alive and honoring them in everything we can do. Do it for you, do it for them, and the world will be a better place for it.

One of my favorite gospel songs is "Precious Lord, Take My Hand." It's always felt powerful, psychically, and has gotten me through grief in my own life. It was written by a man named Thomas A. Dorsey, who was born in 1899. Recently, I found out the origin of the song, and it embodies the power of channeling our pain into something more. In an interview, Tom said:

> My wife, Nettie, was about to bear our first child. I was called to St. Louis to sing in a revival. I wondered if I should go because of my wife's condition. She persuaded me that I should go ahead, so I, alone in my Model A, drove to St. Louis.
>
> During the first night of the meetings, a lad brought a telegram to me while I was still on the platform. It was horrible news. It was a message that my wife had died giving birth to our son.
>
> I rushed to a phone while the people were still singing and found that the message was true. Mr. Gus Evans drove me back to Chicago that night.
>
> When I arrived I found that the wonderful baby boy was seemingly fine, and yet, that night he also died. I buried my wife and little son in the same casket.
>
> I became very despondent and filled with grief. A few days later I visited with my good friend,

Professor Frye. We walked around the campus of Annie Malone's Poro College for a while and then went into one of the music rooms.

I sat down at a piano and began to improvise on the keyboard. Suddenly, I found myself playing a particular melody that I hadn't played before that time. (It was an adaptation of George N. Allen's melody used with the old hymn, "Must Jesus Bear the Cross Alone?") As I played, I began to say, "Blessed Lord, blessed Lord, blessed Lord." My friend walked over to me and said, "Why don't you make that precious Lord?" I then began to sing, "Precious Lord, take my hand, lead me on, help me stand."

When I finished the song, we began to use it and it has been going ever since. I have gotten letters from people all over the world. It was a great tragedy, but we got the message to the world.

Thomas's tragic loss led to a song that would be a crutch to millions of people decades later. Oprah Winfrey played this very song to her mother shortly before she died, and it evokes emotion few songs will ever be able to come close to. Through our pain, incredible gifts can be given to the world. In order for us to do something with it all, though, we must first let ourselves feel it. You owe it to yourself to grieve. We are all going to be touched by death and one day die ourselves; it's what we do in the meantime that makes a difference. We're all sharing the human experience, the highs and lows and in-betweens.

The idea that we'll all go through similar experiences in individual ways is not a new one. All of humanity has been linked by life, death, and an aim to find purpose in it all. To conclude, this excerpt from *Invisible Helpers* by C. W. Leadbeater, published in 1889, reads:

> When the last shred of the personality is gone all that can thus suffer has passed away, and in the perfected Adept there is unruffled peace and everlasting joy. He sees the end toward which all is working, and rejoices in that end, knowing that earth's sorrow is but a passing phase in human evolution.
>
> . . . Let no man therefore despair because he thinks the task too great for him; what man has done man can do, and just in proportion as we extend our aid to those whom we can help, so will those who have already attained be able to in turn help us. So from the lowest to the highest we who are treading the steps of the path are bound together by one long chain of mutual service, and none need feel neglected or alone, for though sometimes the lower flights of the great staircase may be wreathed in mist, we know that it leads to happier regions and purer air, where the light is always shining.

6

Recognize the Signs

"In every moment, the Universe is whispering to you. You're constantly surrounded by signs, coincidences, and synchronicities, all aimed at propelling you in the direction of your destiny."

—Denise Linn

Humanity has always looked for signs of guidance from the great beyond. Equally, mankind has always felt called to interpret certain occurrences as spiritual or heaven-sent. Signs are calls to focus. They alert our attention to something important or meaningful. I've learned from my work that signs have at least two meanings: 1) the message in the sign 2) the timing of the sign. Whether it's a dream, synchronicity, or vision, the content of the experience is just as important as the timing. Sometimes, timing is a message in itself.

Historically, mankind hasn't attributed signs to a single source. Biblical prophets attribute signs as messages from God. Spiritualists often attribute signs as guidance from spirits or spirit guides. My take is that it really doesn't matter who exactly the sender of the signs is. To me, it's all an extension of a higher power. The guides, deities, and spirits of time past may all be utilizing a Godly means of communication. I consider a message from a loved one to be God-sent. No matter what your exact views are on the sender of the signs, I encourage you to not let that mystery get in the way of noticing them. In all of the readings I've done, I'm certain that spirits have the ability to send messages. I also have found that spirit guides are capable of bringing certain signs to our attention. Equally, one may attribute spiritual guidance to angels or discarnate beings.

John Keel, a famous paranormal investigator and author of *The Mothman Prophecies*, had a lot to say about the spectrum of phenomena that encompasses the sign-senders. After decades of research into paranormal experiences, he created the concept of the superspectrum. The superspectrum is an all-encompassing term that refers to the underlying fabric of the universe from which all normal and paranormal things stem. All of what we would define as supernatural exists in this superspectrum. Like all spectrums, there are classifications or levels. Just as a belief in multiple spiritual planes permeates religion and spirituality, the superspectrum is a magnification of this idea. About the superspectrum, Keel writes:

> God or the God-like force would be at the highest point of the superspectrum; energy vibrating at an incalculable frequency, storing all information in negative and positive charges, and operating

with an intelligence so refined and so all-encompassing it defies description. Like a computer, it would be without compassion or emotion as it manipulates all the physical components in the universe from microbes and ants to whole galaxies. It would be capable of changing frequencies at will, descending down the spectrum, manipulating energy masses into the lower EM [electromagnetic] spectrum, creating matter, even living things, from energy.

. . . loathsome things, and shining angels would all be its handiwork, its way of reaching down and communicating with us . . . They would come from outside time and space, forever repeating the cryptic statement: "We are One."

To Keel, the superspectrum was an explanation for a wide array of unexplained phenomena that has plagued humanity since its beginning. He believed it may have gone on to inspire myth and religion. Certainly, experiences outside our means of understanding have created entire belief systems. Religion has been our way of trying to explain the truly unexplainable. As with William James and his four characteristics of a mystical state, we understand that by default, mystical experiences defy description. Religion has been an attempt at explaining the source of the paranormal, but descriptors fall short. The fact that ineffability, or being beyond words, is a characteristic of all mystical experiences reflects to me that we're not meant to understand it all. We're meant to listen.

John Keel's idea of the superspectrum may just be another attempt at explaining the unexplainable, but the gist of it resonates. The idea that we live in a multidimensional universe and that this plays into spirit communication makes sense. Most experiences deemed paranormal share many of the same characteristics, despite being attributed to drastically different origins. Proponents of the interdimensional theory argue that consciousness could transcend our single dimension, with some consciousnesses having the ability to traverse them at will. This would explain the quick, overwhelming, and immersive nature of most supernatural reports. It materializes into this realm and then disappears into somewhere else. I believe time will reveal that there are greater dimensional aspects at work, and that it's simply a part of how the universe works, like gravity or electromagnetism.

If there is an interdimensional element at work, it would explain how departed consciousnesses seem to have an awareness of their own individual experiences and often understand living people's whereabouts. We're limited in our Earthly perspectives, but they are not. The sign-senders are able, from where they're positioned, to get insight about our world and, sometimes, share it with us.

Signs take shape in a number of ways, the most common being happenstance or synchronicity. (Carl Jung defined synchronicity as "a meaningful coincidence of two or more events where something other than the probability of chance is involved.")

In order to effectively feel our loved ones' signs, it's important that we understand how they best communicate. In readings, departed individuals use symbolism to deliver messages, since it helps relay complex ideas through simple imagery. Outside of readings, that same idea applies. To better understand this, I keep two things in mind:

Our departed loved ones have a far higher understanding of the interconnection of all things in a way that we don't feel in this realm (in part due to ego). Symbolism can be universal, and it paints a picture of what's being said, while communicating big-picture ideas with less effort. This explains, I believe, why many people feel connections with butterflies, doves, or feathers. All three of these things share the same symbolic representation: transcendence, taking flight, and boundless freedom. If you see and attribute these symbols to your loved one, it's likely that within that sign lies a reminder they want you to have: they're okay and "above it all." Our loved ones don't give us signs unless there's a message behind that sign, and sometimes people are so desperately searching for a message that they lose sight of the one right in front of them. Even if we don't fully understand the signs we receive, our loved ones are communicating the importance of feeling their continued presence in our lives.

Many people attribute finding dimes, or seeing certain repeating numbers, as a reminder from a loved one that they're still around. I don't believe that our loved ones are following us with rucksacks full of quarters, strategically trying to get our attention with a coin toss. With that said, our departed loved ones are aware of the occurrences we attribute to them and find comfort in. If they know you'll attribute coins to their presence, they may be responsible for helping you notice certain things at certain times, despite not physically placing them there. They can use this understanding to validate their presence, by helping us notice signs they know we'll attribute to them.

Signs can be received from a multitude of sources, both internally and externally. Individuals who are alerted of a loved one's death via premonition experience a sign mentally, without any external factors. In one case, I did a reading for a client and it was revealed that the moment her mother died, every water faucet in the house turned on. This would be an example of an external sign, or one that can be witnessed firsthand by multiple people. Signs work through nature, using both the natural world and our natural states to communicate. Sometimes, these experiences can be frustratingly solitary, happening only when a single person is watching. Other signs involve large groups of people and can be particularly validating.

One incredible example of this happened on a day when I wasn't doing readings at all. I was doing a series of new interviews with La Toya Jackson, to discuss our previous reading together. Connecting with Michael Jackson was a once-in-a-lifetime opportunity, and La Toya was excited to share our time together with the world. I was happy to see La Toya again; it was the first time we'd seen each other since I'd read her at her home and we'd hit it off. She reminded me that in our initial session, I'd mentioned that Michael communicated through the flickering of lights.

La Toya verified that since her brother's untimely passing, she would notice a specific series of flashing lights occur at bizarre times when she felt Michael was around. She was even asked about this by a journalist as we sat together.

After our series of ten interviews was over, it was time to leave. Though there wasn't a reading that day, I could still feel Michael's presence from sitting with La Toya for the hours that it took to do the interviews. When I left, I thought about how odd it would be if he communicated with her in some way after talking about him so much.

Sure enough, on my way home, my phone lit up with calls and texts from various people I'd just said goodbye to. They were on the set cleaning up, and the lights in the building started flashing intensely! When I spoke to the people who were there at the time, they said that, completely unexplainably, the lights above them began glowing and then undulating in brightness; this repeated several times. Both La Toya and I found comfort in the idea that Michael was letting everyone know he was still a part of the production.

I didn't have to be in the room as the lights were flashing to be profoundly affected by the sign that was sent. It was just too much of a coincidence. Similarly, I believe that we should find comfort in signs that are received by other people, even if it doesn't happen in our presence. Very often only certain family members will dream of departed loved ones, while others won't at all. Sometimes, only one person in a family seems to notice signs from loved ones. I believe that the reason for this is a mixture of our concentration and receptivity, and the spirit's ability to communicate. I've observed that sometimes spirits have a harder time communicating with loved ones who are newly grieving and in a deep state of emotional distress. Sometimes, people only notice signs once they've gotten deep into their mourning process. All too often, as with our intuition, we shrug off meaningful moments because they're hard for us to understand. When something doesn't fit into our paradigm of thought, we tend to overlook it and move on. This is why signs can be missed, and some individuals may not notice signs at all.

Many of us have had experiences, myself included, where we acknowledged that something was weird, and moved on without giving it a second thought. In fact, our brains are built to notice mostly what we're expecting to see. Only when we're entirely present can we intuit the full scope of what's in front of us. Considering most of us aren't able to be ever-present, we often miss the full picture of what's going on around us.

My work has shown me that every person has access to greater guidance. Our inability to recognize signs doesn't mean they don't exist. I've seen through my work that when we can better understand the nature of heaven-sent messages, we can notice them more keenly. Intuition is a valuable synchronicity detector and can help us notice things we normally wouldn't. We must ask ourselves: what informs us to look up at certain times? What motivates us to notice one thing and not something else? What is the pull that leads us to certain observations? The answer is intuition.

Sometimes, signs don't require our intuition at all to be understood. They can be clear-cut, obvious, and profoundly puzzling. When such spine-tingling events occur, it can be easy for individuals to put the experience up on a mental shelf and never think about it again. In my work, I've found that thousands of people have had truly baffling experiences involving signs and divine intervention.

The scope of signs is vast, and I've seen some signs firsthand that were equally chilling and validating. One such incident happened to my family while on vacation. Shortly after my grandmother's death in 2006, my family needed a break. We went on our first vacation in a long time to one of my favorite places, Lake Tahoe. We were all looking forward to hiking, canoeing, and taking in the pristine beauty of the mountains.

On our way to the check-in desk at the hotel, we passed by a kiosk of activities. We talked about how fun it would be to try rafting or mountain biking. My parents checked in to the hotel, and I was struck by the realization that this was the first time I'd genuinely been excited for something since my grandmother died.

I went to bed early that night to get ready for the next day ahead, and my parents followed suit. Then, out of nowhere, I woke up to a blaring ringing in the darkness of the room. My mom groggily fumbled for the hotel room landline and picked it up.

"Hello?" she murmured.

"Barbara wants to go with you," the voice on the other end responded.

"There's no Barbara here," my mom retorted.

"She wants to go with you," it repeated.

Click.

The caller hung up. My mom was confused and shocked. Barbara was my grandmother's name.

We assumed that the front desk must have called the wrong hotel room with a message, but the more we thought about it, the stranger it seemed. Although it was a spiritual wake-up call, it wasn't a literal one. It was in the early morning, long before anyone should have been calling a hotel room at risk of waking everyone up. The voice on the other end didn't say hello; just the message, with total confidence. The person on the other end made no effort to explain the meaning of their message. And then they hung up.

If the voice on the other end was indeed someone working at the front desk, they likely had no clue the significance of what their words meant. If it really was just a mix-up in rooms, that meant that the potentiality of signs involving and using people was present. Whatever the case, I was deeply comforted by the experience, albeit startled. How often do you get what feels like a phone call from heaven? In life, my grandmother worked as a telephone switchboard operator for thirty years, connecting people to talk with their loved ones. I like to think my grandmother's spirit was out there somewhere, orchestrating one final call to say she wanted to come along.

We can become recipients of messages, and sometimes deliverers of them ourselves. Unwittingly, we can find ourselves in positions in which our own actions seem to inform a greater purpose. One such instance happened at a time when I was deep in my grief process. At the time, I was mourning the death of a close friend and wanted to go back to a place we'd had childhood memories. This place was the Cayucos Pier, located in a sleepy beach town on the central coast of California. My friend and I'd spent many summers running around and getting into trouble as rambunctious teenagers. When he died of cancer, his name was honored on the pier with a plaque. When we arrived at the pier, I was surprised to find that this wasn't a unique memorial. If I had to estimate, I'd say there were about two hundred plaques that lined every few inches of the long wooden structure that extended into the ocean.

As my partner Clint and I stood at the base of the pier, I told him about my surprise that there were so many plaques, discouraged in my knowingness that we'd be there all day trying to find the one honoring my friend. Without saying a word, Clint grabbed my hand and we walked down the pier. We didn't speak, walked too fast to even look at each individual plaque. He seemed like a man on a mission, and so I quietly followed him. We got a ways down the pier, only for him to stop abruptly. His back was turned to the plaques, but his arrival to this one spot was almost instinctive.

Instinct it was. As I took a closer look at the plaque behind him, I was stunned to realize that he was standing only inches away from the plaque dedicated to my departed friend. On the plaque, along with his name, was a quote to the effect of, "His memory reminds us to make the most of every day, and enjoy every sunset."

This moment was a personal validation for me. I was used to being the one to guide people to messages from their loved ones, and here my boyfriend was guiding me to the exact spot, despite both of us being none the wiser. In that moment there was an interesting role reversal, and I felt a bit like how people feel when they get a reading!

Whether we're subjected to signs or become a part of their delivery, the mystery continues. There are times when messages have literal multidimensional meaning, and there's layers to the message. There are times in readings when I feel called to acknowledge a specific event that ends up holding extreme sentimental value to the person I'm reading. In this way, my message acts as a sign in itself.

One such example occurred in my reading with Dave and Odette Annabel. I read them together at their home, and we had a lovely afternoon connecting with a number of loved ones. Dave's grandmother came through with particular persistence, acknowledging a whole laundry list of specific details. Towards the end of the reading, she communicated that she was watching over their baby, who she never got to meet when she was alive. To further validate this fact, she had me tell Dave to "Check the baby monitor!"

It's very rare that I get yelled at from the other side, but her insistence didn't go unnoticed. I confidently brought this message through, to Dave and Odette's bemusement. They knew exactly what that meant, they said. Dave proceeded to pull out his phone and tinker with it for a few moments, revealing a baby-monitor app on his phone.

He went through a series of saved recordings and showed me one recorded shortly before our reading. In it, it was evident that it was nighttime, and their baby was sleeping soundly in the crib. As the baby slept, a light appeared in the corner of the frame. Then, the light grew larger. It floated with a sentient quality over the child's head and seemed to linger by its shoulder. Then, to everyone's surprise, a voice was heard on the baby monitor saying, "Hi, Grandma."

It was chilling footage. The fact that it was so insistently referred to in the reading was a sign in and of itself. The Annabels knew that Dave's grandmother was watching over the baby. Yet, she made it a point to extra-verify by delivering the message to me. I wondered if the grandmother knew her spirit was recorded, or if she was just regularly making visitations to their child's bedside. In any event, I felt like a messenger of signs even more than usual.

Many people notice signs at certain times and certain places. Often times people will notice activity before they go to bed at night, or when they're in a more relaxed state. Most often, people will experience activity in places familiar to them, like their home. It's easier to tell what's abnormal activity when you're in an environment you know like the back of your hand. Countless reports of strange activity exist today, with people keeping their stories quiet out of fear of ridicule. Because I'm a medium, people feel comfortable telling me about their experiences, and they're abundant! Electrical malfunctions and missing objects happen surprisingly frequently. Reports of bedside visitations or strange experiences while one is in bed are common. Oftentimes people will say that when they're going through a particularly stressful time, signs and activity seem to increase. My greatest takeaway from hearing so many stories is the importance of the timing of them. So often there was greater meaning to the experience when put into the context of when it happened. Uncannily, signs were often noticed when the person either needed guidance or was unaware of something that needed to be brought to their attention. Signs usually exist to either reinforce that we're not alone, or they act as a call to action for us to do something differently. Signs can comfort and inspire and help us make change inwardly and outwardly. These moments of guidance are invaluable, but their duration is usually short. Being able to glean their wisdom is pivotal to spiritual growth and can transform us with the knowingness that we never walk alone. Truly believing that, and having evidence of it through signs, lays a foundation of belief that cannot be wavered. The experiences reported to me, and the ones I've had firsthand, have all reiterated the fact that we're part of an interactive world. Departed loved ones have the ability, in some cases, to intervene and help us. This may be dependent ultimately on the spirit's journey and progress, but it's evident that such experiences do happen.

As we've covered, sometimes living people become sign-senders from the beyond, even if they're unaware of it at the time. Because the departed have a more heightened understanding of our interactions, they may inform certain decisions that people make. If they want us to receive a certain message, they may utilize other people's intuition to alert us to our own. In one spooky example, a woman I read was grieving the death of her brother and reported the strangest occurrence of her life. Her brother was a massive Pittsburgh Steelers fan, wearing a hat with their signage everywhere. In life, his family joked with him that it was odd he was such a die-hard fan, considering he'd grown up in southern California. He just liked the team, and it stuck out. On the day of his burial, it was decided that it would only be appropriate to bury him with the hat he wore so frequently. After the service, my client went home and spent the day responding to the outreach from loved ones. She was deep in her grief, but she wanted to carry on with some normalcy.

So, she ran by the grocery store to pick up a few things, still wearing the black clothing that adorned her at the service only hours prior. When she walked through the front door of the building with her cart in hand, she was trying to not stick out. She'd been answering phone calls and dealing with visitors all day, and she just wanted a moment to herself.

As she turned down the aisle, she had to get past just one person. It was a man with a Steeler's baseball cap, identical to the one she just watched her brother get buried in. She was struck by the similarity of his appearance, and spent a moment staring at him. When the man noticed her, he did something she wasn't expecting. He made eye contact with her, and briefly tugged on his ear two times. What the man didn't realize was that this was an inside gesture between my client and her brother. Since childhood, they communicated "I love you" with two pulls to the earlobe. The man getting groceries probably had no clue of the extent his actions jolted the woman that stared at him. She left the experience with an uncanny feeling that her brother was behind her seeing the man and his recognizable action.

Something similar happened to my mom and me only recently, and it's the closest I've ever had to a firsthand run-in with that type of a sign.

Shortly after my lung collapsed in early 2020, I was in and out of the hospital and not at my best. I went from doing readings nearly every day, to all of that coming to a screeching halt as I faced weeks in the hospital. During this time, I was given such heavy pain medicine that it was very hard to concentrate, let alone do readings. For a few weeks, I didn't feel like a medium. My body and mind were in recovery mode, and all of my focus was on healing myself.

So, you can imagine my surprise when I was visited by a departed loved one of my own during a dream. It was my mother's niece—my cousin, Karen, who died prematurely after lifelong health issues. My cousin was in and out of my childhood. She was too old for me to really relate to, but young enough that my mom still took on a protective role for her. In some sense, my mom treated us both like her children.

When Karen fell ill with a compromised immune system and kidney failure, my mom and I accompanied her to dialysis and spent time with her in her final days. I was always struck by how unique her appearance was: her olive skin and uniquely bright eyes were matched with a husky voice and almost masculine demeanor. She had lived a tough life, and was tougher from it. She had a childlike energy and viewed my mom as a mother figure.

When Karen visited me in a dream during my hospital stay, I was shocked. Though we were somewhat close, I hadn't heard from her spirit since she'd died, and assumed she'd never visit. In the dream, she was simply smiling, and she looked visibly healthier.

Then, I woke up. I was in the hospital bed and my mom was only feet away, asleep on a recliner the nurses brought in for her. We were both alerted by a knock on the door, unsure of who was coming in.

"Hi, I'm Karen and I'm here to take your trash," a voice said.

The woman who entered was fumbling with a new bag for the wastebasket, and she came through the door back-first. When she turned around, I was stunned.

Her resemblance to our Karen was uncanny. Her complexion, facial features, and even eye color were all the same. Most of all, her voice was identical to Karen's. It was sweet and singsongy, but a little rough at the same time. I'd never heard a voice like Karen's until that moment, and I haven't since.

More strangely, when the woman looked up after greeting us, she stopped in her tracks. When I tell you we were all stunned for probably different reasons, I can't stress the absurdity of the situation enough. She stopped fumbling and stared at my mom, her mouth literally agape.

"You look just like my mom," Karen said.

Tears welled up in the eyes of the woman who was just making her rounds. It was clear her mother had passed, and she was emotionally affected by my mother's presence. We all had to resist the urge to not hug each other in what was an unexpectedly surreal moment. They took a moment to look at each other, none of us saying a word. I knew my mom saw the uncanny resemblance and the synchronicity of the entire situation. The woman assigned to clean the room was meant to walk into the room that day. The entire experience, I believe, was our departed Karen's way of further validating her presence, and maybe the woman's departed family had a hand in bringing her to my mom. During a time of serious health troubles, Karen was lending a familiar face in a way she knew we'd understand. Just as I was there for her in her last days, she was using the living to tend to my side. In this way, living people become an extension of the other side—doing their work, and being part of synchronicities themselves. This incident gave me a profound insight into the nature of synchronicities, and the fact that they can involve the living just as much as the departed.

Oftentimes, synchronicity and coincidence are used interchangeably when they shouldn't be. A synchronicity is defined as a meaningful coincidence, or one that relays profound information. Coincidences happen all the time, and I believe that fact reflects an interconnected universe. We live in a statistical world, and sometimes events converge. Whether there's a mystical component to all coincidences is up for debate. If you believe in pre-determination, then all coincidences are God-inspired. Regardless, synchronicities are undeniably mystical. They stir deep feelings within us and give us an insight into moments when the universe communicates with us directly. Synchronicities can be acknowledged or shrugged off, but they can't be ignored from public consciousness. They'll continue to happen whether they're noticed or not.

Synchronicities are signs, and sometimes they lead to more signs as they are acknowledged. Synchronicities may be the language of the Universe, how it communicates with us. Happenstance, fate, and coincidence guide humanity one meaningful moment at a time. As I've discussed in *Between Two Worlds*, I had a number of precognitive dreams as a child that held relevance for my future. These dreams acted as powerful landmarks for guidance, and helped me know what to look out for to know I was on the right track.

One particularly poignant dream seemed to repeat itself, night after night. In the dream I was standing on a life-size chessboard, where two large pyramids stood beside one another. In the dream, I could feel myself yearning to get to the top of one of the pyramids, as if they represented something I badly wanted to accomplish.

Years later, I walked into a reading at the top of a

notable building in LA. To my shock, I was walking onto the scene of my childhood dream. I couldn't hide my shock from my client, who was very weirded out by the fact that I was so moved by the setting of our reading. I knew the moment I saw the scene that there was something important about that day in my life. It ended up being one of the most transformational days of my life, because after my reading I went to my next appointment at the home of a producer for the first time.

That producer would go on to become the executive producer of *Hollywood Medium,* and my longtime manager. He changed my life. I knew I was on my intended path when a dream from my past catapulted me into the future it was guiding me towards.

Dreams are an invaluable resource for messages and insight. Equally valuable is the conscious state you enter before you fall asleep. This transitional state can evoke pre-dream imagery that can be remembered later on. Why might one do that, you might be wondering? Well, this state gives us a glimpse into our unconscious minds. The part of ourselves that is usually hidden, even to us, comes out in our restful states. We notice more when we're still. I suspect this may even be why people tend to notice paranormal happenings at night, versus during the day. When we're in a relaxed state, unstimulated by our usual beeps and buzzes, we notice more. In the late hours of the evening, we're a lot more receptive to subtleties that go unnoticed throughout our day. This state of pre-sleep is a resource into our inner worlds.

This is something you experience nightly: the state between wakefulness and sleep, referred to as "hypnagogia." This method of inspiration helped Aristotle and Edgar Allan Poe intuit their most profound contributions.

We don't usually remember the random sounds and images experienced in this in-between, yet these impressions are valuable insights from the unconscious. If you pay enough attention, you'll find the hypnagogic state to be full of creative and intuitive epiphanies.

Frankenstein author Mary Shelley wrote in the early morning, saying, "I saw with eyes shut, but acute mental vision."

Beethoven and Thomas Edison both found meaning in the ideas evoked while dozing off. It's known that Albert Einstein took twenty-minute naps to facilitate his "aha!" moments. As a medium, I see and hear the departed most clearly while on the verge of sleep. It's as if there's something purifying about going into a slumber, enabling deeper layers of consciousness to be revealed.

Cambridge University researcher Valdas Noreika says, "When we enter sleep, the brain steadily dismantles the models and concepts we use to interpret the world, leading to moments of experience unconstrained by our usual mental filters." You can imagine how helpful this is to receiving psychic insight, untarnished by our conscious minds and opinions. When it comes to readings, not overanalyzing is crucial, and this state leaves no room for analysis during the experience, only afterwards.

One of the challenges of signs is identifying their meaning in the present. Hindsight is 2020, but in the moment, it can sometimes prove difficult to get the message. When someone proves to be unwholesome, we often kick ourselves for not going with our initial gut feeling that proved to be correct. Only after we've received corroborating information do we often look back and realize that a part of us knew the truth. This is why intuition becomes helpful, as it shows us which coincidences are synchronicities and what's worth really paying attention to.

The reality of coincidences and their relationship with us is vast. Coincidences, and to those who could recognize their meaning, synchronicities, have shaped humanity in every way. Our lives are guided by the turns we make throughout it. Ripple effects of change radiate from a single moment, changing the greater unit it is a part of. One such example can be seen in the fact that World War I was started by a literal wrong turn.

In 1914, stability in Europe was beginning to crumble. Those who were paying attention in history class know that World War I was started by the assassination of Archduke Franz Ferdinand and his wife by a Bosnian-Serb nationalist. This one event led to the deaths of seventeen million soldiers and civilians.

Frans knew of the risk of assassination, as there were multiple threats. He decided to go forward with a trip to Bosnia, well aware of the potential security risks. Despite this, he traveled in an open car, and their motorcade route was public knowledge well beforehand.

On the morning of June 28, 1914, seven would-be assassins waited along the expected route and prepared their weapons. They strapped themselves with explosives and wielded handguns and cyanide pills in the event of their capture. As the vehicle made its way down one of Saravejo's most popular streets, a noise rang out.

A Bosnian Serb named Nedeljko Čabrinović threw a bomb at the car. The driver suddenly swerved out of the way, and the bomb damaged the vehicle that was trailing behind. Talk about a close call! At this point, most level-headed people would have been spooked by nearly being bombed to death, but Archduke Franz Ferdinand wasn't that kind of guy.

After going about his political duties in town, he asked to make one final stop at a hospital to visit an injured military official. The driver of the car was told to go a specific route that was deemed safer, but the directions weren't understood. The directions were spoken in German, and the driver spoke Czech. This single snafu changed the world.

As the car turned onto Franz Joseph Street, it sped to the exact location of Gavrilo Princip, a would-be assassin who happened to be waiting underneath an awning at a general store. It was the wrong turn that would change the course of history.

An occupant in the car berated the driver for taking the wrong route, and then shots rang out. Both the Archduke and his wife were shot at point-blank range, purely because of a series of unfortunate events. Two gunshots changed the course of history, and only one month after Franz Ferdinand's death, Austria-Hungary declared war on Serbia. Thus began four years of world-altering chaos.

As embodied by this example, little things lead to big things. One small spark can kindle magnificent change. Our actions have immediate consequences, while simultaneously creating change in ways that aren't evident at the time. When we're faced with reminders of the synchronistic nature of things, we don't always know what to do with that information. It usually gets shrugged off at worst, or acknowledged at best. I've had a number of these experiences throughout my life, and have seen the power of signs and timing in the lives of clients.

One such example happened when I bought my first home. The day that I got the keys, I walked around the property and took in the surreality of being a home-owner. My property has two buildings, a main house and a newer side-house. As I walked into the side-house and absorbed the excitement of the situation, I was struck by how familiar everything felt. It was as if I had some cellular memory of the structures, and I took a moment to bask in the feeling.

As I had a moment of deep gratitude, I opened my eyes and was looking beneath a staircase. Squinting, I looked closer as I noticed what looked like writing on the side of the wall. I walked up closer to it, only to realize that a date was stamped into the wood that the building was made of. The date? January thirteenth. My birthday! In that moment, I had chills throughout my body and was tickled by the coincidence. I took it as a sign that the house was made for me!

Interestingly, birthday and anniversary synchronicities seem to be common. They are, after all, dates that represent so much more than just a date. They're symbolic for continual themes in our lives, and that which we hold sentimental value around. One such case happened to a client of mine who was house-cleaning on her birthday.

Her grandmother had died years prior, and as she cleaned her house, she consciously thought about how her grandmother used to take her to the store every birthday to receive any one gift of her choosing. The memories made her smile, but she didn't think much of it beyond it being a cherished experience.

That was, until she found an envelope with her name on it. As she was rummaging through old papers and books, she opened a Bible that she hadn't seen in years. When she opened the book to its spine, an envelope fell to the ground. As she looked closer, she realized it wasn't her handwriting—it was her grandmother's. She became emotional at the possibility of it being an unopened letter, and as she tore the top off, she was greeted with an old birthday card.

HAPPY BIRTHDAY! I LOVE YOU!—NANA the note read.

My client was stunned. Her grandmother must have sent her the card years prior, with it simply going unnoticed. It hid in the Bible until the exact moment, years later, that it was opened and revealed. Her grandmother was able to get her message across, even if it was years late. This further validates that the timing of a message is sometimes a message itself.

As we've covered, synchronicities and signs are part of nature. Though they are often regarded as supernatural, signs can come from a multitude of places within nature. Sometimes, people receive messages through animals or natural events.

The day I was set to read Jim Parsons, he reported that his home was inundated with hummingbirds. The idea of animals being messengers for the spiritual realms isn't a new concept, as seen in many Native American beliefs. Notably, one of the "haunted" locations I was asked to investigate years ago was riddled with bad energy. I was never able to determine the cause, but was shaken when I walked to the structure only to be met by an angry horde of bees. It was as if they appeared out of nowhere, buzzing angrily as a clear message that I needed to leave.

These concepts might sound "out there" to people who aren't familiar with nature's role in the "supernatural," but animal messengers are a historic part of universal communication and warrant a closer look.

In 2012, Lawrence Anthony, deemed "The Elephant Whisperer," died at the age of sixty-one. A lifelong, dedicated conservationist, Lawrence had taken care of and rehabilitated countless elephants. Though the elephants and their keeper hadn't interacted for a year and a half leading up to his death, the animals seemed to instinctually know he died. They trekked for over twelve hours, in two herds, walking solemnly in a sort of funeral precession. They arrived at his home, stuck around for two days, and then dispersed back to where they came.

Science has no explanation for how a group of elephants could sense their former caretaker's heart stop from miles away. This case is a profound example of how interrelated we are, and the power that love has in transcending species and communication.

The founder of the term synchronicity, Carl Jung, experienced a fascinating validation involving nature. Bernard D. Beitman, M.D., author of *Connecting with Coincidence*, writes about Jung's creepy-crawly coincidence:

> A young woman of high education and serious demeanor entered Jung's office. Jung could see that her quest for psychological change was doomed unless he was able [to] succeed in softening her rationalist shell with "a somewhat more

human understanding." He needed the magic of coincidence. He remained attentive to the young woman while hoping something unexpected and irrational would turn up. As she described a golden scarab—a costly piece of jewelry—she had received in a dream the night before, he heard a tapping on the window. Jung opened the window to synchronicity. He plucked the scarabaeid beetle out of the air. The beetle, which closely resembled the golden scarab, was just what he needed—or just what she needed. "Here is your scarab," he said to the woman, as he handed her a link between her dreams and the external world.

As you can see, synchronicities seem to respond to intentions. When we're conscious of what they are and open to being guided by them, our worldview can change. Even the most hardened of skeptics might be surprised by their own potential to pull back the curtain into a world not known to them. Furthermore, signs have shaped human culture and provided moments of divine intervention since our inception.

If you're like me, you might wonder what mechanisms are at play behind the synchronicity phenomena. While the consciousness of departed people certainly influences some synchronicities, I'm doubtful that they're responsible for all of them. It may be possible that what we call synchronicity is actually more than one phenomenon at work. Coincidence may be a higher means of communication, to beings other than ourselves. Those in spirit realms seem to have an altered, interconnected understanding of the world. This understanding may inform how they communicate with us, through symbolism and time.

John Keel's *The Eighth Tower* has an insightful quote about how other consciousnesses may view things differently than we do, and be more capable than we are:

> The ability to see the future. People with this ability are not just tuning in to other human minds; their brains are somehow tuned to the superspectrum itself, and they are tapping the information stored in it. The future already exists in the superspectrum.

The easiest analogy to this phenomenon is to compare the superspectrum with a boy with a microscope. When he peers at a drop of water on a slide he is, in a sense, looking into another world quite possibly separate from his own reality. In thirty seconds of his time, he can watch an entire life cycle of a microbe—its birth, its multiplying, and its death. Because of its very small size, if the microbe had a sense of time, those thirty seconds would seem like thirty of our years. Time, as Einstein observed, is not a real measurement—but is relative. The microbe swimming about in his drop of water knows nothing about the universe outside his immediate environment, and the boy exists in a whole different dimension.

One wonders to what extent signs can change the present and influence the future. If linear time in its entirety exists in some superspectrum-type realm, it may be all happening simultaneously. This idea can send us down a rabbit hole of complex thinking that will get us nowhere fast. As much as I try to understand the foundation of synchronicity, it evades me. I understand who and what may be responsible, but the phenomenon itself seems to surpass time and space. From my work, I've considered the possibility that the future has some influence on the past. In physics, this concept is called retrocausality. It's one of many potential explanations for why premonitions and signs transcend our understanding of time.

Consider this famous example of a future event being intuited. In Buddy Holly and his wife's case, the future had a very profound impact on their present. One night in January 1959, the famous singer and his wife both awoke from individual nightmares. His wife stated that in her dream, she watched a fireball hurdle towards the ground at her. It roared past her, leaving a crater in the scorched earth. Buddy was struck by his wife's nightmare because he, too, was having an airplane-related dream. In it, he and his wife were in a small aircraft, and she was ordered off the plane. They understood in the dream that they had to be apart from each other, though Buddy recounted telling her, "Don't worry, I'll come back and get you!"

Buddy died in a tragic airplane accident less than a month after the eerie coincidence. It was clear that some force was at work, communicating to the couple of the events that were to come. Both individuals were struck by the nightmares enough to share the incident with those around them. In this case, the future and past collided in a brief insight into inevitability.

This story might make you question: if the couple had put enough weight into their dreams so as to not fly on planes from thereon out, could they have saved Buddy's life?

I don't believe so. I've seen too many indications that there's some design behind when we're born and when we depart. The times we live in require our consciousness to be in them, and when our role in our time in history is done, we pass away.

This idea is reflected in countless reports by near-death experiencers, who almost universally acknowledge understanding the sentiment of "it's not your time." Whether the experiencer is told this by a spirit or the presence of God, or just has some telepathic understanding, this report is incredibly common.

This leads me to believe that the phenomenon wants us to know that there's a purpose behind why we're here when we are. Why would it go out of its way to tell us it's not our time to die? The fact that the sentiment is expressed at all indicates that there is a significance in the timing of our passing.

Whether a sign comes in the form of a dream or a synchronicity, signs play into our conscious and sub-conscious experiences. They're often symbolic. They communicate higher concepts and complex ideas, through simple but jolting moments of serendipity. Signs are the validation of our relationship with something greater than ourselves. When they happen, they affirm the mysterious and interconnected nature of all things. While many would like to discount these experiences, they're ingrained in the human experience. They'll always be a part of us, and a portion of the population will benefit greatly from their assistance. Divinely inspired experiences will pass the test of time, if history has anything to say about it. They've shaped people's beliefs and motivations and have subtly guided humanity down a path of purpose ingrained with meaning.

We understand that signs manifest in dreams and in our waking life, through synchronicity and symbolism. When a coincidence is meaningful, it may alter our behavior more than we realize. Receiving a sign feels nice, but more than that, it evokes an existential realization that there's more to the universe than meets the eye. Some people are cripplingly afraid of this idea and shut down their openness to the subject altogether. Others, like myself, find comfort in these guiding insights that remind us that we're never alone.

It can be easy for some to embrace one worldview about the origin of signs, while ignoring others. I think one must look at all the ways the universe has historically communicated with us in order to get a clearer understanding of the complex phenomena at play. While we know that spirits are responsible for some coincidences, others might be from a higher power. Our guides, whoever they may be, may also influence the signs we're called to notice. Trying to grasp the origin of all the sign-senders is a futile effort. I believe it's simply too complex to understand and encompasses many different sources. Trying to understand it all can be likened to the struggle of the blind men in one of my favorite stories, "Blind Men and an Elephant."

This fable tells the story of six blind men who come across an elephant. Because of their limited perception, each man touches a different part of the elephant and is certain that what they are feeling is the whole animal itself. One man holds the tusk and declares the whole elephant to be a spear, another man holds the tail and insists the elephant is obviously like a rope. Yet by feeling only one part of it, each man only had a limited understanding of what the elephant truly was. Each man had a unique perspective, also known as a narrative. As human beings, we have as many narratives as we do opinions about the world, and they're often incomplete . . . like the blind men touching the elephant.

We can only really understand our interpretation of the truth. Though we may all possess different aspects of a greater truth, no single interpretation paints a full picture. Whether you believe signs are from spirits exclusively, or angels, or God himself, they all have value. We don't have to understand something for it to be real and profound.

I've had a number of experiences that've made me challenge my thinking and consider new possibilities. Considering dreams have been such a meaningful way for me to receive messages, one dream in particular stood out for its absurdity. I couldn't write it off as eating too much before bed, either, because it reoccurred. In the dream, I was in downtown Hanford, an area I worked and did readings in as a teenager. Cars rushed down the street, and I was across the street from a park near the courthouse. As I waited at the crosswalk, a strange sight unfolded. What appeared to be a large coyote or wolf-like creature emerged from behind a pillar and walked in my direction. It crossed the street, and I was struck by how it appeared to be walking in slow motion. The first time I experienced this dream, I knew I was dreaming, but couldn't wake up. In what felt like the weirdest episode ever of *Clifford the Big Red Dog,* I proceeded to cross the street and follow the creature into the park.

It led me to a very random spot in the park near the police station. As we quietly walked together, I didn't communicate with my newfound furry dream-friend.

It suddenly stopped walking and looked directly at the ground in front of it. As I looked closer, I saw a large red "X," and a massive treasure chest overflowing with gold coins. It was ridiculous. It felt like my dream state had combined leprechauns with *Pirates of the Caribbean*. All that was missing was the end of the rainbow!

And then, I woke up. After this happened in a succession of nights, my curiosity got the best of me. I went to downtown Hanford, determined to find out what this bizarrely childish dream could mean. I waited at the crosswalk as I'd done night after night, only this time while awake. I scanned the park from a distance, trying to figure out if there was anything notable in the direction of my dream. As I crossed the street, I could already tell there wasn't much to see at the spot of the "X." A patch of grass near an old civil war cannon, I'd walked by it countless times. No one was in the vicinity, and all that I could see was a shimmery material strewn about on the ground. I looked closer, and was immediately amused by what I saw. On the ground in front of me was a deflated balloon with the initialism LOL on it. Seriously? I stood back with a chilling sense that I'd been messed with. I wanted my pot of gold!

In all seriousness, the absurdity of the situation wasn't lost on me. I've noted since then that the coyote archetype can be seen throughout many cultures. "The Trickster," as the coyote is known in Native American theology, has been known to appear to many people. It's informed myth and even been popularized in media (I'm talking to you, Wile E. Coyote). Carl Jung believed that the Trickster was an entire archetype of the human unconscious, and that humanity has formed myths around it. Whether my dream was the result of a mischievous spirit or my own unconscious, I'll never know. It wasn't particularly meaningful, but then again, maybe the meaning was to use discernment in what I attributed meaning to.

I use this as a cautionary tale, in the sense that it's important to not try to find too much meaning in signs. In our attempt to find deeper meaning, we may lose the surface layer meaning. It's important to take things for what they are; nothing more, nothing less. If I'd shown up to the park with a shovel to do some digging, I'd have been sorely disappointed. If a message is from a loved one, you'll most likely be inclined to know what it means, or at least notice it. It may not be an instantaneous understanding, but if it's intended for you to receive it, you will. Those who are inclined to see meaning in every little thing run the risk of spinning out. It's important to maintain a firm grasp on reality, with the understanding that sometimes reality communicates with us in ways not entirely understood. Trying to understand it all is the human way of approaching spirituality, but it defies being comprehended entirely. This is the nature of reality, and that mystery is by design.

I think of an ideal life as being one that is in alignment with the source. The most meaningful way to live is to be a vessel for greater purpose. When we can know when to go with the flow and when to instill our will, lives transform. Life's balance of push and pull isn't for the faint of heart, but intuition softens the blow. Striving for contentedness may get us further than aiming for perpetual happiness. We can find contentedness through applying our intuition to challenging situations. When we can intuit the lesson in the obstacle, we can hurdle past it into new heights. So many people feel cut off from the spiritual side of themselves and wish to feel the guidance others talk about. Only when we can better know ourselves can these doors be unlocked, and this is why self-awareness is so essential. It's key to knowing what to notice, and when to not look into something too much. Through approaching life intuitively and logically, we can practice maximum efficiency. When we can go in the direction we're guided and heed the signs, we spend less time having to figure it all out on our own. These valuable experiences can be witnessed firsthand by anyone, and setting your intentions to bring forward signs is a huge first step. Truly opening yourself up to the possibility of being communicated with assists in communication.

In conclusion, there's a multitude of possibilities that become realized when we see the spiritual nature of reality. We may not ever be able to fully know our place in it all, but we can use the assistance available to us. Intention is the underlying principle behind prayer and all ritual, and it has profound effects on the world around us. Before there is action, there is intention. Before every reading, I say a prayer to be able to communicate.

As is true for most things, some people are more predisposed to success than others. Some may have to work harder to get the results someone else could achieve in half the time. There's absolutely nothing wrong with this, as all spiritual pursuits require diligence. We're all working with different strengths and areas which we can improve upon. Harness that which you notice, and answer the call of what pops out at you. The coincidental nature of reality can provide us with valuable insights, and it helps to be aware of them. It's probable that there are those who heed spiritual signs and reap great fulfillment, without ever even realizing the spiritual nature of their hunches. Wall Street traders and Tibetan monks alike acknowledge the power of intuition. It exists within all of us, waiting to be cultivated and developed for our betterment. Depending on our intentions, signs can guide us in the direction we're destined to go.

Life is a series of doorways. One door opens, another closes. Grace can be found in knowing when to stay, and when to walk through the next door that awaits us. The only guarantee in life is change, and we're served to better cope with it. Intuition, synchronicity, and the spiritual nature of reality remind us that with every door we walk through, we are not alone. Through times of hardship and unpredictability, there exists somewhere out there a force that's on our side. Every personal struggle and intimate moment of suffering is seen by something else. You are never alone in your pain.

Matthew 7:7 says, "Ask and it will be given to you; seek and you will find; knock and the door will be opened to you."

Those words are as true now as they were when they were written. There exists an abundance of guidance waiting to be unlocked in every moment of stillness. When we're quiet enough to hear the whispers of the universe, we're reminded that we're all on the way to the same destination. We never truly depart from the love we share and make on this Earth. These windows of opportunity to connect with our highest potential exist to help us. As we go through life learning how to more effectively love ourselves and others, signs act as the roadmap of where to look next. Living spiritually is just as much about trust as it is about faith. We must have faith in that which we cannot ever truly understand, and trust in factors greater than ourselves. As we all navigate our journey Home, my wish for you is continued guidance. May you find answers in your own empowerment, and the inner keys to walk through every door that's yet to come.

7

Clairvoyant Q&A

This chapter will provide an update on what I've come to understand since the publishing of *Between Two Worlds*. In my first book, I answered some of my most frequently received questions. This Q&A will act as an update to that one, as I've had an array of new and insightful experiences in the past few years. I've always emphasized that I learn something new with every reading, and I'll do my best to share with you what I've gleaned thus far. If what I've come to understand is ever altered by new information, I'll always make it a point to share how my views have changed. In the following pages, I'll elaborate on old questions and answer new ones.

My aim is to share with you my observations and opinions about what I've deduced from my spiritual work. I don't claim to have the answers to all things, and the more I learn, the more I realize the limitation of belief. I can only infer from my experiences with the understanding that my views are ever-growing and evolving. The foundations of my beliefs are solid, but their intricacies are deeply nuanced. I hope you'll use this Q&A as an opportunity to delve into these topics and decide for yourself what you resonate with.

Have your readings informed your belief in God, and if so, what is that belief?

As I've said before, my upbringing was a religious one. As I've grown older and had to rely on my intuition more through readings, my spirituality has evolved from a faith-based system to a trust-based one. As a child, I sat in pews for hours, being told to have faith in that which I could not see. Faith was a testament to our belief in God. However, as I began to harness my spirituality, I realized faith wasn't the only way to acknowledge the divine. Trust was even more fulfilling. I could trust in my ability, and I knew it came from something greater than myself. This trust changed my relationship with a higher power, and made the reality of it a lot more tangible than faith alone could provide.

I view God as the source of all things. I liken religion to a language that we use to communicate with the divine, depending on our culture. If you're born in India, you may be raised Hindu or Muslim. If you're raised in the Deep South of America, you might be a conservative Christian. Where we're born, when we're born, and the religious beliefs of those around us shape our views on faith. I don't believe there is a single right or wrong faith; all are different paths to the same destination so long as compassion is a priority. Religion acts as a snapshot of doctrine from a particular point in time. It's interpretive. As we've discussed, the true nature of mystical experiences transcends words. We're just left to try to explain the unexplainable and lend meaning to that which we cannot fully comprehend. This is religion.

God, to me, exists both outside us and within us. The spark of life that we all possess comes from somewhere. Consciousness may in itself be a reflection of our origin. It's made clear to me that there exists a collective consciousness, a single all-encompassing unit of which we're all a part. Our consciousness comes from, and is an extension of, one thing. This one source may be the intelligence that created the universe or that, at the very least, permeates all conscious experience. When we worship God through religion, we're utilizing a belief system to surrender to something greater than ourselves. I think it's important to not downplay that we are an extension of God. Just as this source has both constructive and destructive capabilities, so do we.

What qualities do spirits consider important for us to implement in our lives?

Countless spirits have acknowledged the importance of going with the flow when resistance is futile. Life is a balancing act between knowing when to lean in and opt out. We're always having to decide what to prioritize, and thereby what warrants attention and what doesn't. Our lives are heavily nuanced by our beliefs about our lives. Many of the hurdles we face are complicated by our own thoughts. Our ego can magnify manageable issues to the point of complete chaos. Humanity's lack of overall self-awareness has led to a lot of mindless action, with no awareness of the consequences. Until death, that is. Those on the other side acknowledge the importance of consequential thinking and of being mindful of the power our thoughts and actions wield. Humans are prone to speak carelessly, or act in ways that aren't in alignment with their true intentions.

Know yourself. Know what intentions you hold and why you hold them. Always ask yourself why you have attachment to certain thoughts or circumstances. Identify how your conditioning has affected your motivations. What makes you feel alive? Why is that? What prevents you from doing more of it?

Consciousness in the next realm understands the importance of self-discovery. This only happens through asking important, and sometimes difficult, questions. When we strive to know ourselves, we better know the world, and live more well-rounded lives as a result. When we can go inward and see all we have to offer, we can maximize the potential we have. Everyone should make an effort to explore the worlds that exist inside them.

How can we better understand intuitive development?

Intuition is inner insight through discerning thoughts, feelings, and knowingness. If we recognize that intrinsic knowledge informs our dreams, bad vibes, spontaneous decisions, and near misses, then we understand intuition. Not only does it wave red flags and signal danger, intuition also inspires new ideas, groundbreaking insights, and revolutionary ways of thinking.

All humans ebb and flow with their inner-tuition. Sometimes we're in tune with our inner worlds; other times the outer world takes precedence. When our intuition flows consciously with our intention (or will), we are spiritually en rapport with the source of all intuition, the collective consciousness. Like any skill, talent, or sense, what's practiced becomes prominent.

Every invention, composition, and innovative idea has come from somewhere. That somewhere is the collective consciousnesses. We come from and will someday return to this universal godhead whose existence permeates our own. The "other side" represents a state we all ultimately obtain, and in this state, we recognize unity as humanity's greatest purpose. The impressions and clues we're able to decipher reflect that intuition as the higher basis of all reasoning. All intuitive glimpses, personal or profound, move humanity in the direction of gradual understanding.

The Trinity of Intuition

All great epiphanies, personal or profound, start with stage 1: an initial starting perspective, then stage 2: a sudden epiphany, and finally stage 3: a conviction that what was realized is true. This is the trinity of intuition.

Having an intuitive hunch isn't unusual, and it happens to us all the time. Stage 3 is where people run into problems, and that's often because we're conditioned to ignore hunches that aren't deemed rational. When we can see our intuition through stages 1 through 3, and get out of our own way, progress is made.

Most of us at some point have experienced glimpses of intuition. This originates from the unconscious and works its way up to our conscious minds. Some people believe in a superconsciousness, which is a direct link to the source of all information. The idea is that intuition may pull from this God-source of information that embodies all consciousnesses. This may explain why certain intuitive insights can be gleaned about other people, and why many psychic experiences involve feelings of taking on experiences as if they are the intuitive's own.

In people with a strong identification with inner knowingness, like children, intuition can seem clearer. Adults often have a hard time identifying the inner worlds because of self-doubt, ego, and confirmation bias. Like languages, intuition is most easily retained by children and becomes increasingly difficult as we get older. As we get set in our ways, seeing past our ego becomes harder.

Think back to when you were in school and the teacher presented the class with a question to be answered. So as to be the first to be called on, you confidently raise your hand and shout the wrong answer. Those with the most conviction are bound to misrepresent what's intuited. Harnessing your intuition requires the confidence to recognize what's known on a deeper level and bring it to the surface. Equally, too much confidence without discernment and perspective renders the process void. It's a fine line to ride, but an essential balance.

Relying on self-belief alone creates a lack of context that can lead to overzealous certainty and harmful disillusions. People who identify staunchly with their own beliefs run the risk of shutting out intuition altogether. Those who perceive themselves as having control over their inner-knowingness fall victim to their own beliefs about themselves. It's important to remain open minded, and ever humble. The great irony is that courage is required to identify and materialize intuition, but if courage becomes cockiness, ego destroys intuition.

What are your thoughts on the Law of Attraction?

The Law of Attraction has become a huge facet of the New Age community since the publishing of *The Secret*. Endorsed by Oprah, *The Secret* claimed to give insight into a process of materialization used by history's greatest minds. It harkens back to the New Thought Movement, and the idea that intention alone can create change in the physical world. There is certainly relevance to the idea that intentions have power. They're a predecessor to action and breathe life into what we do. Prayer and ritual are merely actions that are done with the hope of magnifying an intention. Setting out intentions to communicate with higher forces certainly has relevance, and I don't argue the power of prayer in some cases.

However, the Law of Attraction seems like watered-down spirituality. The idea that concentration alone can materialize what we want seems like wishful thinking. I don't dispute that vision boards and goal-keeping are an incredible way of keeping us on track and reminding us of what we want. I do not believe, however, that intention alone gets us where we are in life.

The Law of Attraction can seem victim-blamey. It argues that every problem, be it financial, interpersonal, or health-related, can be changed if you intend enough. If your circumstances don't change, you're left to think that you just didn't concentrate hard enough. When it does happen, you attribute manifestation as the cause. Those who come up in underprivileged circumstances shouldn't be blamed for where they are in life. If getting everything we ever wanted was as easy as concentrating, children in Africa would have clean water and no soldier would die in battle. The trend of the Law of Attraction has ebbed and flowed in popularity over the past few decades. My hope is that it can be used in a practical way, without making unrealistic promises. Visualization is powerful. Setting your intention can make ripples in the real world. Yet, it's so much more than just closing your eyes and thinking a happy thought. I fear that the recent New-Ageification of these concepts may take away from their true use.

Do spirits give us any advice on how to more easily forgive others?

As we've covered, forgiveness is a powerful tool in ensuring other people don't live rent-free in your head. By being able to forgive, you cut a cord that ties you to that person unnecessarily. Spirits emphasize that forgiving is not forgetting, and if anything, the life review process makes them face every aspect of who they were and what they did. Forgiveness is a means of freeing ourselves from being re-victimized by them.

Even with this understanding, I still have to work on my grudge-holding. I'm a Capricorn, after all! It's not that I don't forgive, I just believe in healthy boundaries and really commit to them. I believe every single one of us should value our time and our presence in people's lives. Not everybody deserves what you have to offer. As a child, I was notoriously an only child, in that I wasn't always the most diplomatic during playdates. I had to learn the importance of letting things go, and it's served me as an adult. Forgiveness is essential. If you don't have it, you're hurting yourself more than anyone. We must take away the notion that forgiving means forgetting. If anything, spirituality proves that accountability exists, as our soul lasts forever.

I've found that with clients, writing letters is a good start to forgiveness. There's something powerful about being able to put our words on paper and articulate them in a way that we can revise and better understand. Writing things down breathes power into them. Speaking them, even more so. You don't have to reconcile with the person you're having trouble forgiving; that may not be healthy. It may be essential that you and they never speak again. If this is the case, write them a letter anyway. You won't send it to them, but that's not the point. The goal is to express how you feel, recognize it on paper, and hopefully move toward processing your emotions. If you do this, the person never sees what you had to say if you don't want them to.

I'm a huge proponent for extending the olive branch and reaching out. Life's too short to hold onto grudges, but that can be easier said than done. I think the best way to resolve conflict is direct communication. Talk it out. If things get heated, find an objective intermediary to help keep the conversation on track. It may be uncomfortable to talk to someone who has hurt you, but through this discomfort you might glean useful information. You may get clarity from their perspective, or at the very least have your own reinforced. Either way, communication is key. If you aren't able to communicate to the person that's hurt you, writing a letter or keeping a journal is a good start. Other than mushrooms, nothing grows in the dark. When we bring to light what's causing us pain, we purge ourselves of resentment and get on a path to forgiveness.

Have your views changed on monogamy from what you've learned from the other side?

In all my readings, spirits acknowledge reuniting with loved ones from their Earthly lives. This includes former spouses, and sometimes, people have multiple ones throughout a lifetime. This presents interesting questions: do people reunite with all of their spouses, or just some of them? In other words, if someone has multiple spouses, do they reunite with all of them, or just the first one?

I get these questions a lot, and even spirits seem to find the concept amusing. I've done many group readings where a grandmother will acknowledge being reunited with all of the husbands that died before her. I used to spend time as a teenager at Zsa Zsa Gabor's home, and she was known to have nine husbands! When she passed, I was amused at the thought of the lineup that would be awaiting her.

Simply put, departed consciousnesses don't hold marriage in the same regard as we do here. Till death do us part is said for a reason; it doesn't really seem to extend in the way that we know it there. Because our ego is heavily processed, the need for marriage kind of dissipates. Additionally, marriage is more of a legal contract than anything, and there's no need for that when we've departed.

Most importantly, it's acknowledged that love lives on. Platonic love, romantic love, any exchange or expression of selfless compassion has worth. Its value continues on through eternity, as we're reunited with those we loved and those who loved us. Technical definitions of relationships matter on Earth, undoubtedly. It's how we better understand the terms of our connections, and how we present ourselves to the outside world. Spirits may not need to prioritize this anymore, but that shouldn't stop us from getting married, staying single, or doing whatever works for us so long as it's healthy and brings harm to no one.

What can spirits teach us about self-love?

The death process reveals to us the true nature of many things. This process gives us an insight into other people's perspectives, their states of mind, and why they did what they did. When we're given this understanding, it's a lot easier to let things go. Resentments, misunderstandings, and frustration are all processed when we understand why people did what they did. It may not make it right, but it allows us to see the reality of situations that were diluted by our own ego.

When we're able to have this same understanding with ourselves, dramatic change occurs. Life review processes give us insight into how we handled things, just as much as they give us insight into how others did. Just as we must come to terms with others and their actions, we have to come to terms with our own. So many spirits acknowledge that shame, guilt, and critical self-talk plagued their lives. The narratives we form about ourselves are sometimes skewed heavily by trauma and pain avoidance. The life review process strips back the layers of lies we tell ourselves, and also the things we dislike most for the silliest of reasons. We can take hints from this life review process and implement them into our lives while we're still here.

When we realize that our beliefs about ourselves define our ego structures, we can change for the better. Noticing areas that trigger us, and striving to better get to the root of the issue, should be a universal goal for all of us. Through self-awareness, we build inner worlds and foundations that greatness can be built upon. Self-love is an essential part of navigating this world and cultivating things that bring you joy is important. In doing this, you can find a greater appreciation in your own accomplishments, no matter their size. Take pride in your ability to do better and strive to always respond compassionately. We all fall short, but extending the same kindness to ourselves as we would a friend is important. The self-talk you tell yourself should motivate you to do better, not feel trapped in your own head.

Do you think birth order makes a difference on intuition?

In my work, I come into contact with a lot of intuitive people. Often, I have the opportunity to delve into their personal lives and hear about their upbringings. I'm struck by how similar all of our stories seem to be. Usually, intuitive people only become intuitive after a life-changing event, like a death or illness. Many intuitive people dealt with childhood illness or deal with chronic illness as adults. I've even seen that birth order may influence whether someone is inclined to be intuitive or not.

As an only child, I spent so much time alone that I was able to go inward and develop that aspect of myself. Interestingly, many intuitives are also the oldest children in the family, if not only children. I've discussed that both nature and nurture probably influence the extent to which someone is intuitive, but this pattern is interesting to me. There may be something about being left to have our own internal experiences at an early age that helps make people intuitive. Some of us may learn intuitive faculties more adeptly than others, due to our childhood circumstances. Whatever the cause, there's a lot of research to be done on the subject, and I believe it'll notice some interesting patterns and characteristics among intuitive people.

Do narcissists have specific spiritual struggles to overcome?

Spirits come through all the time acknowledging that in life, they were narcissists. Some had deeply narcissistic qualities, and others would qualify as having NPD, or narcissistic personality disorder. Souls who navigated this challenge often realize that their personality, or ego, wreaked havoc on their lives. Their beliefs about themselves in relation to others was deeply skewed. They often reflect that they were never capable of taking accountability and always blamed their issues on others. Narcissists have ego structures that create something of an echo chamber, in that they're only able to truly value their own views. In these self-centered individuals there exists a deep sense of loneliness and an inability to authentically connect to the world outside of themselves.

Narcissists, as the legend goes, can be charismatic and self-absorbed. Like the myth of Narcissus, who was so in love with himself that he drowned in his own reflection, these individuals are much more than vain. They're completely self-immersed. This limits a person's ability to recognize themselves in others and see others in themselves. This narrow-minded perspective hinders lesson-learning, and the narcissist often doesn't see the point of it at all. They can't see the forest for the trees, because their time is spent self-gratifying and trying to get ahead.

We've all met a narcissist at one time or another. They can often leave empathetic people in their lives feeling victimized or drained. NPD is historically difficult to treat, and I believe it says a lot about the ego structures we create and enable. The trauma we sustain in life can either hinder us or propel us, depending on what structures we have in place to cope with it all. Self-absorption is a dangerous quality that can make a person so self-assured, they never take others into consideration. We should strive to minimize these qualities in our own spiritual progress and recognize these attributes in those who have them.

Being intuitive requires confidence. But the narcissistic intuitive is bound to fall by their own sword. Discernment is impossible when you're not capable of seeing the relevance in what others bring to the table. The ego structures that maintain self-centeredness are carnal and go against the realization of collective consciousness. If you're only able to see your own perspective, and only able to value yourself, everyone else becomes a nonfactor. This is dangerous to health and spirituality. We must look at the root of what compels us to not see past ourselves, and combat it with compassion.

Do readings ever give an indication as to the purpose of mankind?

I'm still waiting for the day that a spirit comes through and gives me the answer to all of humankind's purpose. I won't hold my breath. If anything, I've found that the subject of purpose is multifaceted and complex. To some extent, we have as much purpose in life as we lend purpose to it. One of the universal purposes we all share is to do better. Consciousness, by its infinite nature, is ever growing and changing. You know more today than you knew yesterday. Purpose can be found in reaping the benefits of lessons.

We might think of ourselves as loving people, but we all have hang-ups and unhealthy habits tied to our ego. Whether they're thought habits or physical ones, we all can improve our patterns. Much of what human beings do is habitual. We handle new issues similarly to how we've handled previous ones, in most cases. We look to the past for guidance about how to handle the present and future. When we can make it our focus to find purpose in every obstacle, our narratives change from a victim-based one, to an empowering one.

As human beings, we're social creatures. I don't believe this is on accident. Our consciousness is compelled to make bonds and is intuitively called to look at others for a feeling of self-meaning. Compassionate acts help us self-realize, just as much as they help others. Through doing activities that help us feel part of the collective, we become less isolated, less purposeless. A true understanding of our interconnection is a purpose I believe all souls have to strive for. In life, we can make conscious strides by analyzing the defensive mechanisms we use to navigate society and improve upon them. When we can find activities that help us obtain inner peace in our outer interactions, we're on the right track to living purposefully.

Also, purposeful living ties directly into mindfulness. When was the last time you ate breakfast without checking your phone? When was the last time you consciously reminded a loved one of how much they mean to you? All of these acts, big and small, aid in feeling a sense of purpose. The more conscious we can be of the inner and the outer, the more we have to work with. Purpose is both individual and collective. We're all here to unblock that which prevents love from getting in. But more uniquely, we're all here to navigate individual struggles and work through certain circumstances. What we retain from it all contributes to learning, and these purposeful lessons are taken with us when we die.

Are introverted people more likely to be intuitive?

I can't tell you the amount of people that have come to meet-and-greets and told me that they, too, have an ability. Usually, these self-identified intuitive people are shy or deep thinkers. They usually have certain qualities that have made them feel socially isolated, or not accepted by others. Intuitive people are usually deeply sensitive to their own emotions and those of other people. To a deeply intuitive person, this world can be particularly brutal. While non-intuitives step on the feelings of others with no awareness, the intuitive person can't help but be hyper-aware of what they say and do.

So, generally, they say less. They realize the impact of their words and actions. Truly intuitive people are usually introverted, because they're in touch with a deeper part of themselves. I don't have anything against extroverts. There're plenty of extroverted mediums. The issue with extroversion is that it can become something of a performance art. People who always need to be the center of attention aren't necessarily coming from a place of prioritizing the group over the individual.

Historically, stoicism is a commonly attributed value to those who are more enlightened. Those who are mindful of their inner world are less likely to project their ego structures onto other people. While the extrovert may be the loudest person in the room, the introvert is a wallflower that observes and listens. The quality of being able to listen is key. Listening to ourselves, listening to our intuition, and listening to the world around us all require silence. When we can see the value in introversion, we can be more mindful. Though our introspective and extrospective qualities usually depend on our environment, I think anyone developing intuition should strive to go inward before expressing outward.

Introversion leads to self-discovery. Introverts often notice what the extroverts don't. The ability to see the power of your word, and use it accordingly, is intuitive. Those who are reckless with their words aren't operating intuitively. There's nothing wrong with being outgoing, and if anything, it's necessary in some ways to have the confidence to do a reading. But there's an importance of balance. True discernment is knowing when to speak and, more importantly, when to listen.

Are you plagued by the presence of spirits all the time?

One big misconception about mediums is that we're constantly bombarded by spirits. People think of mediums, like Oda Mae Brown in the movie *Ghost*, constantly have to fend off otherworldly visitors. Thankfully, I don't find this to be the case at all. There are certainly times where I'll connect with a spirit unintentionally or get a reading when I'm not expecting it.

However, boundaries are a very important part of being a medium. Anyone without boundaries can attest to how draining letting everything in can be. In my work, I've developed healthy boundaries, both with the living and the departed. Doing such allows me to turn on and work when I need to and shut off as needed. In previous instances, I've likened my medium ability to that of a volume dial. To some extent, there's always intuitive background noise. When I go to do a reading, I consciously turn that volume dial up so I can more clearly hear what I need to know. Even when I'm not working, I get residual impressions from every environment I'm in and feel something from every interaction I have.

I don't let this rule my life. I think part of being a responsible, functional medium is being able to have some way to get in tune and then to tune out. I've obtained this through certain rituals that involve prayer and meditation, but everyone navigates these boundaries differently. There are times where I'll be sitting at home with my boyfriend or family, and a message for one of them will come through. In these cases, it's up to me to determine if it's an appropriate time or place to share. Usually, it is.

As a child, I had much less control over what came through. I'd see people standing in my room when I would wake up in the mornings. At school, I'd be over-whelmed with psychic impressions from students and teachers. My inability to recognize my ability allowed it to run rampant in my personal life. Before I really recognized this, I was inundated with anxiety and generally unhealthy.

When I started making a time and a place for readings, life improved. I was able to blow off the necessary steam by doing some readings at designated times, which allowed me to not tune in when I wasn't working. Even still, if I go more than two weeks without doing a reading, I begin feeling poorly. Readings, to some extent, have become something I have to do in order to survive. Like eating and drinking, I have to prioritize my soul's purpose, or else run the risk of neglecting myself. Just like how binge-eating or binge-drinking is unhealthy, so, too, is overexerting intuition. Many people, especially in the beginning of their spiritual awakenings, feel they have little control over what they see and feel. And though I technically am not responsible for what I receive, I do play a role in my receptivity to receive. By implementing certain practices and rituals, people can develop more control over when they receive intuitive messages. This is essential to health, well-being, and normalcy.

When you go to historical places, do you feel all of the departed people that were once there?

One of the most fascinating aspects of being a medium is being able to intuit information about the past of certain places. Because psychometry, or reading intuitive impressions of objects, is such a big part of my work, this adds a new dimension to what I'm able to feel. Being able to touch objects that have historic value can give new insight into old events. On my first trip to London, I was barely able to leave the hotel room without overwhelmingly dreadful feelings. Touching the doorknobs of old buildings and walking the cobblestone streets made it hard to feel present in my body. It was as if everything that had ever happened there was ingrained in the environment. Lives lived and lost through centuries were entrenched in the space around me. It was suffocating.

In London, I had to make a great effort to turn my intuitive volume dial down. I have to do the same when I go to places like New York City or downtown Los Angeles. I grew up in a rural area, and currently live in a sparsely populated place. This has been incredibly beneficial to my health, and I go to great lengths to make sure my environment is as conducive to peace as possible.

In recent years, I've had the opportunity to explore a number of supposedly haunted places. Many of these locations are also historic and have an extensive resume of people who have died on site. I've been surprised how often I go to such places expecting them to be full of otherworldly activity, only to be disappointed. That's not to say that I haven't experienced anomalous events in paranormal places, but I've often left wondering who or what was actually responsible for the reported phenomena.

I had the opportunity to investigate one of the most haunted destinations in America, a pub called Kells in the Pike Place Market of Seattle. The pub had a particularly interesting history of more than one kind of spirit. It was once the Butterworth Building, opened in 1903, known as the first mortuary in Seattle's history. It stood as the Spanish Flu, tuberculosis, and diphtheria ravaged the city, leaving nameless bodies on the street. It was such a systemic problem that the city began offering fifty dollars per corpse as a clean-up effort. A body would be delivered to the mortuary, and twenty-five dollars was given to the mortician. This became a money-making opportunity, and it was exploited in horrific ways. Dr. Linda Hazzard (1867–1938) was licensed by the state of Washington as a "fasting specialist," calling herself a doctor despite no medical certification. She believed that starvation was a cure for all illnesses, and knowingly killed people with her backward treatments. When money was offered for bodies in the street, Dr. Hazzard knew where to find them.

The doctor ended up dying at the age of seventy, due in part to starving herself. The bodies that went through the Butterworth Building may not have all been departed when they showed up. One would think the structure would be brimming with ghosts. When my friend Charlie and I first came upon Kells, we weren't anticipating much activity. We'd just the day before explored Seattle Underground, a myriad of tunnels that exists under the city. Formerly, the passageways were at ground level in the mid-nineteenth century. The entire city of Seattle was elevated after the Great Seattle Fire in 1889. This elevation left the former city way completely unused, and thus it was sealed up into total darkness.

It was a surreal sight, but not particularly haunted. We walked down what felt like miles of windows and storefronts that stood against nothing but dirt. With minimal lighting, we relied on a single flashlight to navigate our way through the underground labyrinth. The only exciting moment happened towards the end of the tour, when I jumped and yelled, scaring Charlie to the point of near tears. She still hasn't forgiven me for that. All in all, Seattle Underground was a bust as far as ghosts went.

So, when we walked into Kells, our expectations were low. When we first walked in, I was struck by a physical heaviness on my shoulders. It was as if the air in the building had a density, like invisible fog. We both noted the weird sensations and continued through the front of the building toward the stairs. As we approached the stairs, I saw a quick shadow out of the corner of my eye. It went in the direction of the tables, and I assumed it was one of the cameramen. When I found out it wasn't, I was a little spooked and ready to go upstairs.

As I walked up the stairs, I had to physically stop. I was struck by a strong mental image of children running up and down the crowded stairway. I had an instinctive reflex to move my knees, afraid that I'd get an elbow to my calves. But there was no one there.

Continuing up the stairs, I began hearing music. I was a little annoyed because the venue was told to shut off any overhead music for the sake of filming. I mentioned it only a little later, and realized that no music had been playing at all. The music was in my head. When I got to the top of the stairway, I entered a room that seemed to be the most likely source of the music. I was later told that the room once housed a massive organ, played for mourners as they awaited funeral processions.

By this point, I couldn't get out of the building fast enough. I was less struck by the odd mental images and sounds than by the feeling of heaviness. It was physically uncomfortable. It felt like being in a space where the past and present seemed to collide, and I wasn't having it. We concluded filming, and it took me a solid week to shake off the weight that rested on my entire being.

I left Kells uncertain of the presence of ghosts. If anything, most of what I witnessed seemed to be residual occurrences from the past. The entity walking to the tables, the children rushing past my feet, and the funeral music all seemed to indicate impressions from decades ago. I didn't have anyone come through, nor did I feel the urge to communicate with anyone. It seemed that all of the activity in the building that I witnessed was purely psychic residue, or experiences embedded in their environment.

In the various locations I investigated, I rarely came away with a feeling of the presence of ghosts. I've come to gradually understand the power that events hold on their environment. Similar to psychometry, or the idea that energy is held in objects, I have no doubt actions leave marks where they happen. Intuitive people, or those who just happen to notice them, may falsely attribute these impressions as being from spirits.

All in all, I look forward to the day that I investigate a haunted place and am met by a spirit. The souls I communicate with in readings seem to be in a higher place, somewhere far from this world. My interest in connecting with earthbound spirits has only been emboldened by my letdowns in other investigations. My greatest takeaway was that hauntings aren't as common as often thought, and every action leaves its mark in the vastness of eternity.

Are there any notable hauntings that you find most intriguing?

For all of the made-for-television movies about "famous" hauntings, it can be hard to discern what's the truth in films based on a true story. *The Haunting in Connecticut* was one of my favorite scary movies as a kid, but the film drastically varied from the case it was loosely inspired by. Similarly, *The Conjuring* weaved a tapestry of fact and fiction, based on the Perron family farm in Harrisville, Rhode Island. In Andrea Perron's three-part book series, *House of Darkness, House of Light,* she details the startling events that plagued the family throughout their ownership.

In one chilling story, Perron recalled a bizarre occurrence involving her mother. In the middle of the night, her mother passed by the dining room and was shocked to see what looked like a family, seated at a completely different dining room table. They seemed engaged with one another and were startled by her presence in the room. The family looked at her in shock, as if they'd seen a ghost. She stared at them back, stunned. In that moment, Perron says, her mother was the apparition to her otherworldly housemates.

It may be the case that some geographic locations possess properties not yet measurable. Places like Skinwalker Ranch in Utah and the Hessdalen Lights of Norway all provide compelling evidence that something not yet understood is at work. The more you look at paranormal phenomena, the more you'll start realizing how similar so many of the reports are. I've come to consider that the worlds of UFOlogy, remote viewing, and mediums are all extensions of the same mechanisms at work. If an orb of light appears in the sky, you might call it a UFO. If that same light appears in your room during a medium reading, you might call that a spirit visitation. The context of the experiences seems to prevent people from seeing the greater commonalities that exist.

Are extraterrestrials ever referred to in readings?

I have yet to connect with an extraterrestrial during a reading. I've experienced a few mysterious instances, like the blue light incident referred to in chapter 1, that've thoroughly baffled me. In such cases, I've wondered if interdimensional mechanisms are at play in certain paranormal phenomena. Certainly, where our consciousness goes when no longer limited to the material world could be considered another dimension altogether.

Of all the theories regarding the origin of unidentified aerial phenomena (UAPs), I resonate with the interdimensional hypothesis the most. Jacques Vallée brilliantly articulates his investigations in a trilogy that spans decades. *Dimensions, Confrontations,* and *Revelations* each explore different aspects of UFO sightings and reports throughout the world. Governments of the world take the threat of unknown lights in the sky seriously and pour millions of dollars into researching them. As of this writing, the Nimitz Pentagon videos are some of the most convincing evidence that something otherworldly is at work. Time will tell the true nature of whatever forces were behind the case.

Jacques Vallée has a fascinating book about how these unexplained occurrences may have informed myths, legend, and some aspects of religion. In *Passport to Magonia,* he eloquently shares the history of UFO experiences and the common characteristics they share. Surprisingly, he found similarities in poltergeist phenomena and many of the characteristics reported by UFO witnesses. Unexplained lights, electrical malfunctions, and mystical qualities are all commonalities the phenomena share.

While some find the prospect of extraterrestrial life frightening, I find it comforting. If there is indeed a watcher out there, it likely holds much more intelligence than any of us. Considering we don't have the technical or theoretical knowledge to know or explain them, they clearly have the upper hand. Their presence puts into perspective that humans are not the highest on the food chain of intelligent life. Taking this reality into consideration is humbling. Whatever the truth, strides are being made to better understand whatever is at work in our skies and among the stars.

Is there any particular set of rituals you do to get ready for a reading?

One of the most valuable tools I've learned to recognize is my ability to make habits. The routines we enact become engrained into our day-to-day lives, and the results can be transformative. For better or worse, our lives are made up of the little things we do repeatedly. When we can aim to view our schedules as opportunities for mindfulness, a chore becomes a ritual. In my own work, I have certain practices that help me get in the proper headspace. Ritual is just a mindful affirmation of intention. Prayer and meditation are both rituals. Creating sacred moments, just for us, strengthens our relationship with the divine.

In the mornings, I try to consciously make it a point to think, "Thank you," as soon as I wake up. Beginning my day with immediate gratitude ensures I don't wake up on the wrong side of the bed. At the very least, it's a reminder of all I have that strengthens me.

Before a reading, I usually become very quiet. On my show, my mom often talks my head off on the way to readings. People wonder if she hams up for the camera, but she's completely how she is when cameras aren't rolling. Despite driving me to hundreds of readings, she's still a Chatty Kathy, or as my dad called her, Chatty Karen. Peace and quiet really helps with introspection and any meditative practice. Shortly before I knock on the door, I enact the final mental process before a reading. I call upon my guides with a short prayer:

> I call upon my guides, angels, and spirit guides to provide precise and accurate information today and always. In God's name I pray, Amen.

Those words are enough to open the floodgates for mental images. As I discussed earlier, some remote viewers listened to music or had certain superstitious practices that helped them tune in to themselves. In my case, my ritual is the short prayer that's preceded over a thousand readings. I believe that when I enact this prayer, my work begins. Evidently, belief may be a huge factor in what propels intention.

Creating a routine of self-care is important. Even if you tell yourself you can't make the time, you can. Everyone can care for themselves when they're going to sleep at night, through processes of meditation and cord-cutting. Making these mental routines a habit might seem strenuous, but after a month of daily practice it becomes second nature. You'll find that you'll call upon the practices you make routine to better cope with life. In this way, the rituals we enact are internal tools that resolve helplessness.

Why do you feel learning is such a central theme in spirituality?

One of the universal concepts of spirituality is that we're here to learn. The idea that life is one big classroom leading up to a final exam is incongruous to some people. The concept of gleaning soul-lessons gets simplified and dumbed down in such a way that seeing lessons in obstacles becomes something of a religion in itself. Why must we learn? Why is it our job to find the lesson in everything? Who signed up for this?

I take an unorthodox approach to learning lessons. I don't view life as a series of tests, nor do I think there's a single instructor providing the opportunities to learn.

I believe that the ability to observe is an inherent part of consciousness. Because consciousness is eternal, we never stop observing. Our observations, by default, help us understand the world around us. The ego structures we create are the filter through which experiences get processed. If we can emphasize the importance of finding the lesson in the obstacle, it can reduce the challenge's hold over our headspace. When we can pull something useful from our challenges, they're not exclusively challenges anymore. I view learning as a by-product of consciousness. We all learn at different rates, and by trying to improve our ego and ourselves, we can learn more gracefully. None of us go through life unscathed. Ultimately, it's what we choose to do with it all moving forward that makes the biggest difference. You can't undo the past, but you can choose what you do with how it defines your future.

All in all, our soul acts as a depository for human experience. Everything we go through, and grow through, strengthens the underlying fabric of our being. This is carried with us forever, which makes short-term challenges seem like just a blip on a much bigger radar. No matter what we go through in the seasons of our life, there is something to be gained. Believing this fully and integrating it into our behavior is half the battle.

Does everybody take accountability when they die?

Yes. Again, I don't believe this accountability comes from a judgmental God, as much as we sort of "judge" ourselves. In life, people's mental filters, conditioning, and ego structures can all skew their ability to empathize with others. People who commit heartless acts often never own up to their destructive actions. It's often the people who should take accountability the most that implement it the least. This makes the death process like whiplash.

Part of the death process involves seeing the bigger picture. With it, we develop an understanding of the constructive and destructive actions we put forth. We recognize the widespread impact every intentional and inadvertent action caused. To those of us who are mindful, self-aware, and kind, the life review process is still a shock to our one-dimensional way of thinking. By default, it's a humbling process. Every single soul that has come forward has expressed a sense of awe around their newfound perspective. These understandings are all necessary and natural and help deconstruct the ego as our consciousness evolves.

I've never had someone come through and acknowledge that they were condemned. The judgements we come to about ourselves and our actions come from a place of self-realization. No matter what conditions prevented someone's human mind from taking accountability, our souls ultimately realize how they changed the collective. We must all face what we've done, and how our inner worlds made change in the outer world.

If you're worried by now, don't be. Those who are worried about their life review aren't the types of people that are prone to having a difficult rebirth into the next realm. It is those that live life mindlessly, hurting people with no regard for compassion, that are affected the most. While I consider death to be an enlightening event for our soul, it is a birth of sorts. Like any labor, there is a process and an initiation into a new form of existence. Cords must be cut, our attachments to our prior world must reduce, and we must acclimate to our new environment.

All of these are universal conditions of the human experience, and the soul follows a similar model in death. Every day we birth new ideas, and every day we experience little deaths. This birth, death, and rebirth cycle allows for learning and change. The extent that we gain from these natural processes is up to us.

Have spirits given any indication as to why the world is in such discord?

People often wonder to what extent spirits care about human matters. Our world is ever-changing, and the tides of progress ebb and flow. Because of the process consciousness goes through upon death, there's an inherent understanding of our path individually and collectively. This clarity reflects a greater truth: we all universally have more in common than what separates us. Our souls are all linked to a common source. Compassion for others is an act of self-compassion. The illusion of fundamental separateness has enabled ego to ravage society.

Ego thrives when it's validated. It creates structures of interpreting the world in a way that elevates itself. It looks to others for reinforcement and preserves itself at all costs. We see unmitigated ego in manifestations of racism and all forms of discrimination. In recent years, we've seen unprecedented protests and racial tensions hitting a fever pitch. This is not an accident.

The collective unconscious of the world is in a balancing act. Despite constant reminders of upheaval from the ever-accessible news, we live in a world that's historically at all-time high in peace. Our access to distressing information has made many assume this discord is new. It is not.

If we view the whole of humanity as a single organism, we get a better understanding of the growth we're watching pan out. Like a child, humanity has had some growing pains. We've had to learn how to walk before we can run and are bound to fall along the way. Mistakes from the past lend opportunities for better behavior in the future. The problem precedes the cure. Humanity as a whole progresses and retrogresses. We take three steps forward, five steps back, and then hopefully six steps forward again. This is how learning happens.

Souls understand this tango with lessons. They see the learning value in mistakes and the importance of doing better when better is known. No matter how staunch the egos of the controlling world powers may be, humanity cannot forget its collective nature. This understanding is intuitive. Ego hijacks this knowingness of universality and creates division through perceived superiority. This battle between collective interests and individual interests is one that plays out before our eyes, daily. It always has.

We live in a tense world. My hope is that these tensions act as a propulsion for positive change, and that it can be harnessed in a way that moves mankind forward. Those on the other side recognize the importance of pressure within the growth process and how uncomfortable change can be. They see the value in speaking truth to power, asserting oneself, and benefiting the collective. Ego structures are involved in all of these steps forward, and through them real change happens.

How can we better cope with the fear of death?

Naturally, I come into contact with many people who are frightened to die. Honestly, aren't we all a little apprehensive? It's uncharted territory, and the single greatest change we go through in our lives. I'm not afraid to die per se, but I'm in no rush to get there. When the time comes, I'll embrace it as gracefully as the spirits have taught me to. We're all going to die, but not everyone is going to live fully.

To those who are afraid of death, self-awareness can help us better understand the root cause. As human beings, we're programmed to want to live. It's the natural way of self-preservation. To be hesitant around dying is, in itself, a safety precaution. However, when this becomes a phobia, our fear of death can limit our life. Is it the possibility of nonexistence that scares you? Is the idea of hell preventing you from living fully? Or is the inherently foreign nature of death an unknown you simply cannot cope with?

Identify the root of your fear; only then can it be worked on. I have an extreme benefit of knowing undeniably that life continues beyond death, but not everyone may be so sure. In these cases, one may fear ceasing to exist altogether. I'd encourage those who have this train of thought to research near-death experiences and the studies that have been done on the subject around the world. The commonalities between reports are too similar to be ignored. Dr. Raymond Moody's body of work has contributed decades worth of valuable research into the continuation of consciousness beyond death.

To some, the idea of hell is terrifying. Deeply ingrained religious beliefs can be hard to decondition, and even some of the most spiritual people are afraid of going to a bad place. While I certainly believe we come to terms with our actions, and in essence judge ourselves in death, I see no indications of a spiteful God.

If this God did exist, I'd have some questions for him. If God has the ability to prevent any evil act, but allows it to happen, is God not responsible for that act? Every sinner and sin would be enabled by this overarching punisher who could step in at any moment. God's apathy towards suffering indicates to me that there isn't a man upstairs with a checklist of deeds and misdeeds.

If there was, he'd have to take accountability for his fundamental role in it all. A chilling quote was carved into the walls of the Mauthausen concentration camp; it read: IF THERE IS A GOD, HE WILL HAVE TO BEG FOR MY FORGIVENESS.

To me, a fear of Hell is illogical. We are extensions of what created us, and therefore it in part is responsible for all that we do. After all, it could step in at any time and prevent wrongdoing if it really adhered to a strict moral code. The fact that it chooses not to says as much about it as it does us.

I see great value in a higher power, but I don't believe in a judgmental God. He'd have to judge himself first to be fair. Souls on the other side acknowledge that we are all works in progress. We don't have to look to another dimension for Hell; it plays out here on Earth every day. While some find the idea of eternal damnation comforting to those most deserving, it's a lazy answer to a complex question.

Ultimately, our souls cannot hide from their impact on others. This understanding permeates every consciousness that comes through. The magnitude of every action is realized, understood, and ultimately processed. I have yet to have a single person come through burning in Hell. Unless they're hiding it from me, I'm inclined to believe the matter is a lot more complex than religion can encapsulate.

To many, death feels like the final frontier. While we have answers about so much of what makes up our physical universe, what awaits us after death is a mystery to most of us. Even those who know of its existence aren't capable of coming close to entirely understanding it. I believe that the key to a peaceful passing is living a life in which there is no regret. Those who have the hardest time in their transitions are those who cannot let go of what could have been.

For this reason, it's important to live meaningfully now. Say it now, do it now, and don't waste time sweating the small stuff. Strive to love people as much as you'd miss them. We're all going to die, but that's a quick process. It's what we do with our lives that should warrant the focus death often gets. Live more meaningfully and create legacies through your actions, as this is a form of immortality in itself.

If my loved one died upset with me, do they forgive me eventually?

Ultimately, they understand you. In life, we're never entirely understood. Who we are either gleans approval or instigates disapproval, and neither are true understanding from others. On the other side however, we see through the judgement calls and understand the true nature of intention. In their journey to peace, the departed have put to rest grudges, resentment, and anger. It serves no purpose where they go.

I've had countless clients who were afraid the departed were mad at them. In one instance, I read for a young woman whose boyfriend had died under extraordinary circumstances. They were en route to a family function and got in a car accident on the way there. My client was driving, and she decided to jerk the car back and forth to jokingly startle her boyfriend. As she did, the car jerked onto loose gravel and she lost control of the vehicle as it sped into a tree. He died instantly, and she was uninjured.

Her regret was immense. Though she left the scene unscathed physically, she was emotionally dead. She couldn't live with the idea that her boyfriend was angry that his life was cut short due to her carelessness. When he came through, I was surprised by his sunny disposition.

He communicated that he understood why she did what she did. It was an accident, after all. Though it wouldn't have happened if she'd made a better judgement call, life is full of fleeting mistakes with unintended consequences. He wanted her to take the opportunity to live more mindfully, to be more present, and to understand the impact of every action. Though he was quite literally impacted by what she did, he was not angry. He had no use for it. His understanding freed her of a lot of the guilt she held onto. She realized that many of the negative emotions she was afraid he felt for her, she actually felt for herself. He was fine with where he was and didn't want her life to end spiritually when his life ended physically.

In most cases, those who are concerned around forgiveness of a departed loved one have to process the emotions themselves. They might be okay with how we handled things, but are we okay with it? We must show ourselves the same compassion we'd extend to a friend, with the knowingness that we are all works in progress. If you knew undoubtedly that they forgive you, would you forgive yourself?

How can I better cope with having views or beliefs
that are different than what's accepted around me?

Many people who find themselves connecting with the other side are afraid to tell their family. Countless people have anomalous experiences they can't explain but know are real. In such cases, it can be difficult to express one's views to friends and family that may think differently. Though I'm lucky to have friends and family who share my train of thought, I face having to explain myself in every interview and skeptical interaction. This has made me keenly aware of my own beliefs and how I present them to those around me.

I've learned that spirituality shouldn't rely on other people's approval. Your spirit is yours, not theirs. Your relationship with the divine is as unique as you are, and just as intimate as your relationship with yourself. No outside force should alter your connection with this deeply intimate part of you. By default, spirituality has always been an inward process.

There's a reason monks throughout the ages were known to be initiated into a great journey, often involving long periods of solitude. Generally, these spiritual journeys are done as a way of strengthening our connection to the divine through introspection. Historically, the journeyer comes back with valuable insight that helps change the world. This, in essence, is the Hero's Journey.

We're all our own protagonist. We're the main character in our story, and our spirituality should be a sacred part of our character. It connects us to that which we cannot see, and helps us feel what's not felt by everyone. The privileged knowledge that spirituality can provide is invaluable, if we're willing to do the work to receive it.

We mustn't rely on the approval of others to see our spiritual selves. Any force that strives to dampen the light we kindle in ourselves is anti-spiritual. Our beliefs don't require us to have large followings, as Jesus only had twelve. What matters is our ability to stick true to what we know and cultivate the divine source inside us all. Those who have transformed the world we live in never feared to deviate from norms. Breaking the mold sets the stage for those who come after us to do the same. So long as compassion informs our belief, we have an endless supply of strength. No matter how different we may be to our surroundings, we're here to improve them.

How can trauma prevent us from moving forward?

As we've discussed, the experiences we go through condition us to react and respond in certain ways. Often, our conditioning is a defense mechanism against prior pain or uncomfortable experiences. We're conditioned to avoid the unpleasant. When we're faced with an exceptionally unpleasant experience, like a trauma, it can negatively affect our ego structures. Trauma can keep us in a rut, prevent growth, and create feedback loops of painful patterns and thinking.

Addiction, abuse, and self-harm are all the result of trauma that goes unresolved. We learn our behavior from somewhere, and our norms are created by what we define them as. This is the power of conditioning, and it can lead our lives into uncharted waters if we're unaware of its influence.

Trauma has a way of making us relive what hurt us. Even though these processes are purely mental, they can take a toll on our mental stamina and physical health. Fear has a way of putting us into states of paralysis, and trauma can keep us underdeveloped and undernourished. I've found that one of the greatest ways to get out of a traumatic rut is to implement a change. Just like our muscles can weaken from disuse, spiritual atrophy sets in when we remain in a stagnant headspace for too long. Trauma keeps us mentally in the past and can make it hard to catch up.

I cannot emphasize the importance of therapy enough. So many people who come to mediums are hesitant to go to grief counselors, thinking a medium will be a cure-all. Our external experiences are only as helpful as our internal narratives are willing to accept, and a traumatized client doesn't lead to an excellent reading. You're better off doing as much internal work as you can to acknowledge and process the trauma, rather than running off to a medium for a quick resolve. Grief counseling can help us lean on an objective source of support and guide us down the unique journey we're on. Every single person can benefit from being honest with themselves and getting the help they need. Though much of spirituality is about going inward, and sometimes journeying alone, we cannot reach our full potential without help. Balancing this dynamic is key. Knowing when to go both inward and outward for support is invaluable. All too often people suffer in silence when resources are there, and all too often people rely on sources outside of themselves for peace. Neither are the way on their own. Rather, we must realize the growth comes from inner work and outer support. Different situations require different treatments, and your willingness to explore all options will help your path. When we see how trauma informs the lens we see life through, we're empowered. Knowledge is power.

What paranormal experiences as a child most informed your beliefs now?

As I was coming to terms with my ability, I had countless brushes with the other side. Each experience seemed to act as a breadcrumb, leading me in a direction of greater understanding. Though I couldn't contextualize my experiences as a child, they grew to serve me in adulthood as I was able to reflect on them. Some of the most impactful experiences I witnessed were incidental, or small validations that reflected much greater truths.

One such example occurred when I was first figuring out my ability. One night, as I lay in my bedroom, I was struck by a feeling of a presence in the room. As I looked at the four corners of my room, nothing seemed out of place. That is, until my attention was directed to the bookcase only feet away. As I watched, a book entitled *Ghosts*, by Hans Holzer, flew off the shelf and landed on the floor beside my bed. I was stunned, and a little spooked. Though it was a small sign, it said volumes! This represented the symbolic nature I would come to understand about spirit communication. Through a little sign, there was a big message. They didn't need to spell it out for me, it was right there in the title.

Just as that experience gave insight into the communicatory nature of spirits, I also came face-to-face with this through profound dreams. Departed individuals would come into my dreams with extreme vividness, and deliver messages that they wanted relayed in my waking life. Not only was I profoundly changed from my grandmother's visitation after her death, but I was visited multiple times by people known and unknown to me. Their messages were always short and spoke to the transient nature of mystical experiences. As short as they were, they were vivid and undeniable. One such example involved my mother's friend who died, and as

I woke up with a message from her, my mom had just returned from her funeral. I didn't know my mom's friend had died, or that she had plans to even attend a funeral, and so this dream reflected a few insights. Not only could spirits communicate in dreams, but the timing of their visitations was a message in itself.

In my early readings, I was struck by how many people shared essentially the same story, varying in minor details. While so many experiencers go through life thinking what they've witnessed can only happen to them, I've seen that much of this is universal. People may not openly discuss the paranormal experiences they have, but they are absolutely widespread. The weight we give these experiences might be a different story, but they exist independent of our belief in them. Dreams, synchronicities, and hunches are all their handiwork. I learned early on that much of what the world deems supernatural and paranormal is natural and normal, just not yet entirely understood. As we speak openly about these experiences, hopefully tides will change in the direction of studying these fascinating, multifaceted phenomena.

Do some spirits remain earthbound, and if so, why?

As I've stated earlier, I've had very few encounters with spirits I'd consider earthbound. It's a rarity for me to connect to any source that's still tied to this realm. The spirits I connect with often feel far away, as if they're calling in from somewhere much more enlightened than Earth. Wherever we go, or whatever state of consciousness we achieve, is an inevitability of all souls. Even to those individuals who are earthbound or don't make a seamless transition, they, too, must cross over eventually. Just as one mustn't get stuck in the birth canal, so, too, we must continue the natural progression of consciousness, even if we fight it.

Cases in which individuals aren't able to transition with ease are rare, but it can happen. Undoubtedly, this is due to situations in which the ego a consciousness possesses isn't ready to give up the reigns. Fear generally acts as an anchor to that which we're afraid of and can hinder our progress on the other side. Granted, most people have some degree of fear before passing, but in most cases, it's relieved and replaced with extreme comfort.

There is a small subset, however, who fight this. Those individuals may be indoctrinated to believe that they're going to Hell, and therefore may fight death tooth and nail. In other cases, individuals may have extremely strong wills and aren't able to let go of the materialistic nature of their reality. Ultimately, it all gets processed and moved on from, but it can keep individuals in a transitory state that isn't the final destination.

If you're worried about becoming an earthbound spirit, don't be. It's generally the ones that aren't afraid of sticking around that end up doing so. We can only fight the natural progression of our soul for so long, but it can be done to some extent.

For most of us, death provides an insight into the meaninglessness of materialism. In using that word, I don't necessarily mean an obsession with material things. If anything, materialism can manifest as an overt attachment to everything physical. Our inability to let go of our surroundings and our physical presence in our loved one's lives can sometimes make the next rebirth more tumultuous. This is why we have a life review, and why our ego is shed, so that we're more able to accept the next state of existence with ease.

I say a prayer for all of the spirits who have yet to find peace. Though they're few and far between, I have to believe that that, too, is part of their spiritual journey. Maybe ruminating on their attachment in this in-between realm forces them to look at what they need to see, for growth. That, too, may be part of some individuals' self-realization process, even if it seems unnerving. The more we can navigate attachment in this life, the more we can let go of it when we die. Through forgiveness we detach from anger. Through trust we detach from fear. Through spirituality we detach from materialism.

Do all coincidences have meaning, and how do we better recognize them?

As we've discussed, meaningful coincidences can give us a glimpse into greater mechanisms at play in the universe. Synchronicities can act firsthand as messages from our loved ones and can help guide the direction of our lives. With that said, not all coincidences are necessarily synchronicities. I believe that the coincidental nature of the universe gives insight into our role in it. We live in a universe of patterns, and sometimes the smallest of coincidences are reminders of this.

This is exemplified in the appearance of repeating numbers. Many people find that certain numbers seem to follow them. Whether it's looking at the time on a clock every day at the same time, or noticing strings of numbers in waking life, all are little indications that there are greater systems at work. We must ask ourselves why certain things get our attention, and what's informing that. I believe the underlying mechanism behind it all is intuition.

Sometimes people message me and are afraid that repeating numbers act as an omen, or that bad news is imminent. I think this is generally a projection of fear in response to something unknown, and we should all be aware of our predisposition to doing this. It's easy to be frightened by what isn't understood, but we must understand that it's as natural as we are. For this reason, it's important to not obsess over little coincidences. They happen all around you, all the time. Sometimes, they give us glimpses into the statistical and interconnected nature of reality.

Carl Jung, the creator of the term synchronicity, reported a fascinating occurrence of this from the wife of a patient of his. What made it so powerful was that the woman had recognized the synchronicity before, identified it, and was able to predict a future event as a result. The story goes:

> The wife of one of my patients, a man in his fifties, once told me in conversation that, at the deaths of her mother and her grandmother, a number of birds gathered outside the windows of the death-chamber. I had heard similar stories from other people. When her husband's treatment was nearing its end, he developed some apparently quite innocuous symptoms which seemed to me, however, to be those of heart disease.
>
> I sent him along to a specialist, who after examining him told me in writing that he could find no cause for anxiety.
>
> On the way back from his consultation (with the medical report in his pocket), my patient collapsed in the street. As he was brought home dying, his wife was already in a great state of anxiety because, soon after her husband had gone to the doctor, a whole flock of birds aligned on their house. She naturally remembered similar incidents that had happened at the death of her own relatives, and feared the worst.

While it wasn't a comforting synchronicity, it was a validating one. Because the woman had been willing to make the mental connection between the flock of birds and an imminent passing, she was able to intuit something that was actively happening. If she had disregarded

the synchronicity as happenstance, the death of her husband would have been more of a shock.

Synchronicities unlock information. Though this can
be a rabbit hole to go down, and one should approach
it with caution, it can be a comforting source of insight.
We mustn't lose our minds and see meaning in everything, but be open to what we notice. That's all. To be
unafraid of recognizing coincidence will help you notice future alignments on your path. All of this helps us
move forward and pulls back the curtain on the interconnected nature of reality.

Acknowledgments

This book wouldn't be possible without the love and support from the living and departed. To every person who ever extended their kindness to me, I owe this book. I honor those who were compassionate just for compassion's sake. So many of these helpers have crossed my paths and lightened the load of heaviness that comes with the territory of being a medium. Personally and professionally, I'm immensely thankful for every person who had a hand in getting me to this point. We're all walking each other home—and I'm glad to be able to walk with you.

I want to thank those in my immediate circle for motivating me to keep writing! My mom and dad have provided unending support and truly demonstrate unconditional love. This is the greatest gift they could have ever given me, and I'm aware of how lucky I am to have them both in the physical world. To Clint, my better half, words will never be enough to convey how much of a pillar of strength you are for me. You always help me ask new questions and revisit old ones.

To my managers, Michael Corbett and Larry Stern, who are the backbone of my professional world and help me share my ability with the world. If it weren't for both of your unique perspectives and ever-helpful input, I wouldn't be where I'm at today. Your support is invaluable, and I look forward to many more adventures together. I also want to thank my assistant Heather Denehy, for being like my second mother (or sister, better yet!). Your diligence in easing so many responsibilities will be forever appreciated. Thanks to you, I'm able to just focus on my job as a medium, knowing that you always have everything taken care of. To Ron, who has departed since *Between Two Worlds*, I know your spirit is in everything I do. This book, and all books, wouldn't have been possible without your love and championing of me.

I want to thank my literary team, Brandi Bowles, Eileen Rothschild, and everyone at St. Martin's Publishing Group. Brandi, you've been with me since day one, and your patience and kindness has been incredible. I'll never forget being chased by TMZ down the streets of NYC with you. Here's to many more books! Eileen, and everyone at St. Martin's, I'm so appreciative to have found a home for my second book. It's been an honor and a privilege to share my story with the world through you.

I'd like to send my gratitude to every medium who came before me, and to those who will come after. As people, we've been persecuted and hunted down for centuries. Only in the past hundred years have mediums felt comfortable coming out from the shadows and honoring their God-given ability. There is still a lot of work to be done, but it wouldn't be possible if not for those who came before us. Every gifted person who was never able to see their ability through, I honor in this book. May we all be inspired to live authentically to who we are, as times change and visibility increases.

I owe eternal gratitude to the guiding forces and spirit guides that've helped me on my path through mediumship. A medium is only as good as the spirit's ability to communicate—and I'm privileged to be able to connect with such fluent communicators. If it weren't for you, my life wouldn't be nearly as purposeful. Your presence in my life shows me that there's always more to life than what's at face value. I hope to continue honoring my ability and do right by what has been given to me.

To the reader, thank you for your unending support of me through the past few years. Coming out of the medium closet wasn't an easy thing to do, but you've all lifted me up and became a second family to me. Navigating life in the public eye has been a challenge at times, but your presence in my life has made it all worth it. Those that cross my path remind me of how much I have to be thankful for, and I'll never forget. To all readers, old and new, I hope this book helps you on your journey. Continue to move forward with the knowingness that you never walk alone, and that we all will meet again.